NORTH YORKSHIRE PUB WALKS

Nathan Vurgest

COUNTRYSIDE BOOKS
NEWBURY BERKSHIRE

First published 2024
© 2024 Nathan Vurgest

All rights reserved. No part of this publication may be reproduced, stored in a retrieval system, or transmitted by any means, electronic, mechanical, photocopying, recording or otherwise, without the prior written permission of the copyright holder and publishers.

COUNTRYSIDE BOOKS
3 Catherine Road
Newbury, Berkshire

To view our complete range of books,
please visit us at
www.countrysidebooks.co.uk

ISBN 978 1 84674 433 4

All materials used in the manufacture of this book carry FSC certification.

Produced through The Letterworks Ltd., Reading
Designed and Typeset by KT Designs, St Helens
Printed by Holywell Press, Oxford

Contents

	Area map	5
	Introduction	6

WALK

1	Coneysthorpe & Welburn – The Crown & Cushion (*6½ miles*)	8
2	Hutton-le-Hole & Lastingham – The Blacksmiths Arms (*4¾ miles*)	13
3	Goathland – The Mallyan Spout Hotel (*4¾ or 5½ miles*)	17
4	Kilburn & the White Horse – The Forresters Arms (*4 miles*)	22
5	Whitby & Sandsend – The Hart Inn (*6¼ miles*)	27
6	Skipwith Common National Nature Reserve – The Drovers Arms (*4½ miles*)	31

7	Danby Beacon – The Duke of Wellington (*6¾ miles*)	35
8	Staveley Nature Reserve – The Royal Oak (*4¼ miles*)	40
9	Newton under Roseberry & Roseberry Topping – The King's Head Inn (*6½ miles*)	44
10	Rosedale Abbey – White Horse Farm Inn (*4 miles*)	49
11	Newton-on-Ouse – The Dawnay Arms (*3¾ miles*)	53
12	Malham – The Lister Arms (*5 miles*)	57
13	Crayke – The Durham Ox (*3 miles*)	62
14	Byland Abbey & Mount Snever Observatory – The Abbey Inn (*3½ or 4 miles*)	66
15	Masham – The King's Head Hotel (*6½ miles*)	70
16	Burnsall & Linton – The Fountaine Inn (*6¼ miles*)	75
17	Hawes & Hardraw – The White Hart Inn (*5 miles*)	79
18	Levisham & the Hole of Horcum – The Horseshoe Inn (*7 miles*)	83
19	Osmotherley & Ingleby Cross – The Golden Lion (*4 or 5½ miles*)	87
20	Kettlewell & Starbotton – The Fox & Hounds (*4½ miles*)	92

KEY TO WALKS:

1. Coneysthorpe
2. Hutton-le-Hole
3. Goathland
4. Kilburn
5. Whitby
6. Skipwith
7. Danby
8. Staveley
9. Newton under Roseberry
10. Rosedale Abbey
11. Newton-on-Ouse
12. Malham
13. Crayke
14. Byland Abbey
15. Masham
16. Burnsall
17. Hawes
18. Levisham & the Hole of Horcum
19. Osmotherley
20. Kettlewell

Introduction

In the course of researching this book, something became clear to me. Yorkshire's nickname, God's Own Country, is more deserved than I'd previously realised.

Beauty, vastness (by our English standards anyway), ruggedness and diversity of landscape – Yorkshire has it all. More than that, there's almost nowhere in the county that hasn't been endowed with at least some of its charm. Stick a pin in a map of Yorkshire and, wherever you end up, I'm confident you'd find yourself within a stone's throw of somewhere perfect for a scenic walk.

I'm not one for major tourist attractions, preferring to venture off the beaten track on a country walk, and North Yorkshire is perfect for this. This is, after all, an area of nearly 3,500 square miles, roughly 40% of which is covered by either National Parks or National Landscapes (formerly AONBs). These are the Yorkshire Dales, the North York Moors, Nidderdale and the Howardian Hills. To the west are the Pennine Hills, and its eastern border is the North Sea. It stretches over 15 miles past Lancashire's most easterly point and only around 10 miles from the west coast.

Spread across this assortment of stunning natural landscapes are innumerable places to go walking. This book's aim is to help you experience the real North Yorkshire through its spectacular countryside and very best pub walks.

The hardest part for me was first establishing the criteria for including walks, and then narrowing down the selection. Some of the routes you find here were selected purely for their beauty, some for their excellent pubs, some for their natural features, some for their location.

I can assure you of one thing – whichever one you choose on any given day, it must be pretty special to have made it into the book.

Nathan Vurgest

PUBLISHER'S NOTE

We hope that you obtain considerable enjoyment from this book; great care has been taken in its preparation. Although at the time of publication all routes followed public rights of way or permitted paths, diversion orders can be made and permissions withdrawn.

We cannot, of course, be held responsible for such diversion orders or any inaccuracies in the text which result from these or any other changes to the routes, nor any damage which might result from walkers trespassing on private property. We are anxious, though, that all the details covering the walks are kept up to date, and would therefore welcome information from readers which would be relevant to future editions.

The simple sketch maps that accompany the walks in this book are based on notes made by the author whilst surveying the routes on the ground. They are designed to show you how to reach the start and to point out the main features of the overall circuit, and they contain a progression of numbers that relate to the paragraphs of the text.

However, for the benefit of a proper map, we do recommend that you purchase the relevant Ordnance Survey sheet covering your walk. Ordnance Survey maps are widely available, especially through booksellers and local newsagents.

Walk 1
CONEYSTHORPE & WELBURN

Distance: 6½ miles (10.5 km)

Start: Coneysthorpe Village Green, Coneysthorpe, YO60 7DD.

Parking: Roadside parking available on Hepton Hill, opposite the entrance to Coneysthorpe village, or around the village green.

OS Map: Explorer 300 Howardian Hills & Malton.
Grid Ref: SE712713.

Terrain: A flat route and mostly easy walking with compact trail surface interspersed with field, tarmac and woodland sections. Dog friendly.

Walk Tips: Plan this walk with enough time to visit some of the surrounding attractions (see *Places of Interest Nearby*), in particular Castle Howard farm shop and garden centre. The deli-style café in Welburn (opposite the pub) is also excellent.

Coneysthorpe & Welburn 1

This flat, easy walk is in the official National Landscape region of the Howardian Hills, a stunning area that skirts the edges of the Castle Howard estate. The route heads from the hamlet of Coneysthorpe to the Crown & Cushion pub in the village of Welburn, mostly following the Centenary Way, through countryside that feels as if it hasn't changed for centuries. Keep your eyes peeled throughout for various impressively grand, historic structures and temples, which are artistically dotted around the impressive Castle Howard grounds.

THE PUB — **THE CROWN & CUSHION** has a large number of tables across numerous, cosy, recently updated yet traditionally styled dining rooms. But the large size of the pub does not detract from its quality as it serves up tasty gastro-pub dishes in a pleasant country village setting. This is a popular pub, so it is advisable to book, especially for Sunday lunch.
☎ 01653 618777   🌐 www.thecrownandcushionwelburn.com

The Walk

❶ From **Coneysthorpe village green**, return to **Hepton Hill** and turn left towards Malton for 100m before heading through the white gate on the right, into a field. You will follow this path for 2 miles, which is part of the **Centenary Way**, a 133km footpath created to commemorate 100 years of Yorkshire County Council.

❷ At the end of this initial field you get your first view of **Castle Howard** in the distance. After ½ mile the track bends round to the left and after 300m ignore the route on your right, which you will use on your return, and keep heading straight on.

North Yorkshire Pub Walks

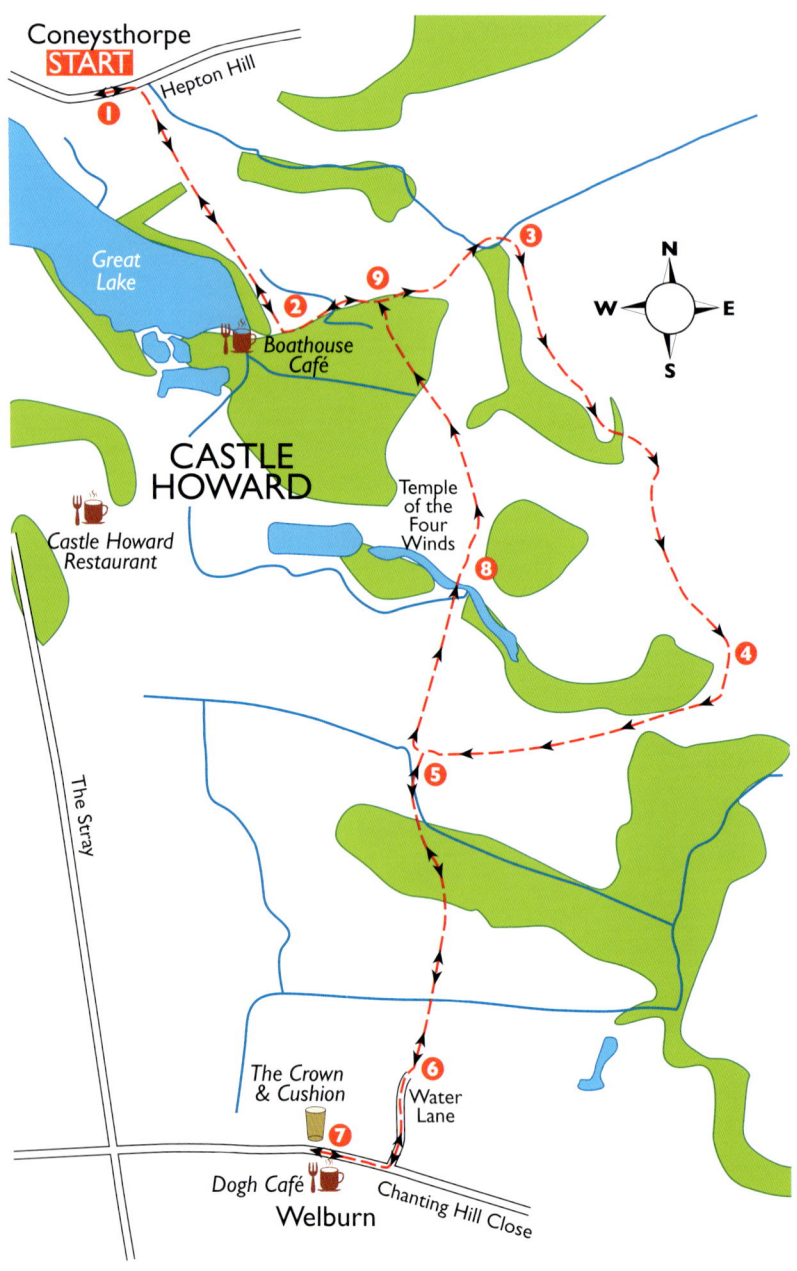

Coneysthorpe & Welburn

3 After ¼ mile bend round to the right and head through the farm buildings. Shortly on the right you can see the **Temple of the Four Winds** on the **Castle Howard estate**. Continue making your way through fields, where the **Castle Howard Mausoleum** appears on the hilltop in front of you. You then reach the next farm, where you bear right alongside pony fields.

4 Head into woodland and then it's another right at a concrete track, signposted Welburn, which carves its way through a large field. As you walk further along this track, Castle Howard itself comes into view on your right, along with **New River Bridge** that you're going to head over on your return journey.

5 Just before the crossroads and signpost, take a left on a grassy track towards Welburn. Pass a bench on the left and head into woodland and then downhill, signposted Welburn. Cross a wooden bridge over **Moorhouse Beck** and head uphill to a gate and field.

6 Straight ahead, you can see the church spire at Welburn and it is now a straight line towards the village, where you will join a road (**Water Lane**) at the end of the field. From here, it's 200m to the village's main road and a right for a further 100m to the pub.

7 Return the way you came, down **Water Lane**, across the field, through the woodland and back to the crossroads in the field at

the back of **Castle Howard**. This time however, instead of turning right, and following the route by which you came, head left then almost immediately right at the signpost. This leads to a stone bridge over a beautiful lake. From the peak of the bridge, you can see a waterfall, the **Temple of the Four Winds** and **Castle Howard** to the left, and the **Mausoleum** to the right.

8 You then head across the field diagonally left, uphill and towards the **Temple of the Four Winds**. After reaching the top of the hill, beside the temple, head towards the dry-stone wall passing the site of the **Temple of Venus** and then follow the clear path along the fence line back into the woodland.

9 In 300m you will reach the path from earlier in the walk. Turn left and then turn right at the next junction, heading across the fields back to **Hepton Hill**. Turn left to return to your car and the village.

Places of Interest Nearby

Just a few miles to the east of the village is the market town of **Malton**, the food capital of Yorkshire. To the west of Coneysthorpe is the village of **Hovingham**, where there is a café and bakery in a beautiful central village setting by the river. Opposite the entrance to Castle Howard is the **Yorkshire Arboretum**, also well worth a visit. **Castle Howard Garden Centre** and the exquisitely stocked **Farm Shop** shouldn't be missed and then of course there is the potential option of entry into the **Castle Howard estate** itself. Lastly, in **Welburn** there is a trendy deli/café, **Dogh**, which serves light meals, and is also a good spot to pick up confectionery based gifts.

Walk 2

Hutton-le-Hole & Lastingham

Distance: 4¾ miles (7.5 km)
Start: Hutton-le-Hole Car Park, Moor Lane, YO62 6UA.
Parking: Hutton-le-Hole Car Park.
OS Map: Explorer OL26 North York Moors, Western Area.
Grid Ref: SE705902.
Terrain: A mixture of grass, tarmac and stone paths with one short woodland hill. Can be wet and muddy in multiple places during the winter. Dog friendly.
Walk Tips: The fields can get waterlogged in winter or wet weather, so it is advisable to wear waterproof boots or shoes.

Hutton-le-Hole is a beautiful postcard-worthy village, with a stream trickling through the centre and a backdrop of sheep grazing peacefully on the green. This is the last outpost before the rugged landscape of the North York Moors just north of the village. This walk takes you across fields and moorland paths to the neighbouring village of Lastingham, a smaller and quieter village away from the droves of tourists in Hutton-le-Hole, where a modern gastro pub awaits.

North Yorkshire Pub Walks

THE PUB — **THE BLACKSMITHS ARMS** in Lastingham has managed to stay up-to-date while retaining a traditional Yorkshire countryside feel. Modern yet quirky décor, a spacious and welcoming beer garden for alfresco dining (if the weather permits) and a central spot in the village are all in its favour.
☎ 01751 417247   🌐 www.blacksmithslastingham.com

The Walk

1 Turn left out of the car park and then left again to join **Main Street** heading towards the village centre and past the **Ryedale Folk Museum**. Opposite the village hall, turn left to follow a public footpath sign heading to the back of the church and across fields. Follow the path through a series of five gates to a metal bridge over the river and heading into woodland.

2 Head uphill along the woodland path and after 100m, a gate opens out onto a path through ferns before reaching a road (**Anserdale Lane**). Turn right along the quiet road, ignoring the

Hutton-le-Hole & Lastingham 2

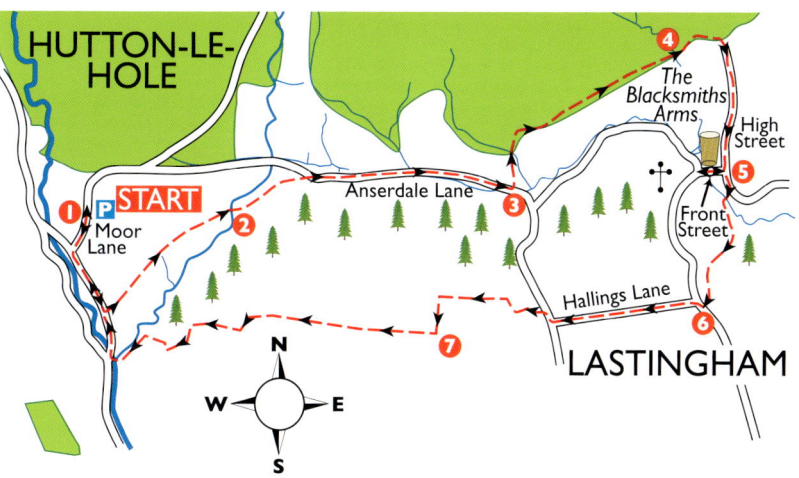

initial footpath sign to the left. In around ½ mile, take the signed footpath to the left, which is 50m before a stone bridge ahead.

3 Head through the gate and continue along the path which follows a fence line, then some wooden signposts, and then a stone wall, before descending downhill and across a stream in just under ½ mile.

4 Head uphill and at a signpost, bench, and Lastingham stone plaque, take a right to head downhill towards the road into **Lastingham**. After ¼ mile downhill on the road (**High Street**), you reach a junction with **Front Street**.

5 If visiting the **Blacksmiths Arms** turn right and the pub is another 50m ahead on the right, opposite the church. To continue the walk turn left on **Front Street** signposted to Cropton. In 50m turn right over the stone bridge and then in another 50m turn right again at a footpath sign. This takes you uphill to a gate and into woodland. It's then a steep 200m through woodland before you reach a road where you can see a black and white signpost to your right.

6 Turn right towards the signpost and follow the road around the left-hand bend towards Spaunton. At the junction follow

North Yorkshire Pub Walks

the road round to the right and then turn left immediately, following the footpath sign and then take the right-hand fork weaving through the farm. Follow the field path towards farm buildings ahead and then turn left when you reach them to carry on along the side of the field. Once past the barns turn right at the footpath sign.

7 Follow the path for ½ mile through the fields as it swings to the left and then right, and then head downhill through woodland. After 200m downhill there is a break in the tree line by a pheasant pen to the right and a gate which you head through. Continue heading downhill following the footpath signs to the river. Turn left through a gate to reach **Main Street** at **Hutton-le-Hole**. Turn right through the village to return to your car.

Places of Interest Nearby

Ryedale Folk Museum is an open-air museum with thousands of objects and where more than 20 heritage buildings have been reconstructed to tell the stories of local people and the area's history from the Iron Age to the present day. In between Hutton-le-Hole and Rosedale Abbey (around a 10-minute drive away) is **Chimney Bank**, one of the steepest roads in the country and worth a visit itself, due to its spectacular views both from the road itself, and on the journey across the moors to get there.

Walk 3
Goathland

Distance: 4¾ or 5½ miles (7.6 or 8.6 km)

Start: The Mallyan Spout Hotel, The Common, Goathland, YO22 5AN.

Parking: The Mallyan Spout Hotel car park, but please ask permission to leave your car.

OS Map: Explorer OL27 North York Moors, Eastern Area.
Grid Ref: NZ827007.

Terrain: The terrain is awkward and rocky for the initial mile along the river's edge. Sure-footedness is needed here, with some clambering around boulders required. When you make it to the road, however, it is easy terrain across fields, forest tracks and road from then on. Only dog friendly if your dog will be comfortable with the initial awkward, rocky terrain.

Walk Tips: There is the option to shorten the walk by heading back from Egton Hole on the more direct route towards the waterfall and your starting position. However, this route won't pass through the centre of Goathland and past the shops and tearoom. The Mallyan Spout Hotel's beer garden is an idyllic spot for an alfresco lunch so it is worth planning this walk when this can be taken advantage of.

This walk takes in the locally famous Mallyan Spout Waterfall, riverside paths through woodland and, finally, rolling hills and farmland. There's the opportunity for a refreshment stop in the

North Yorkshire Pub Walks

pub at Beck Hole, before returning to the centre of Goathland village along the Rail Trail. Goathland itself is well worth a visit; it was the setting for the fictional village of Aidensfield in the *Heartbeat* TV series, and Goathland station was used in the Harry Potter films. Despite its film-star status, this is still a traditional North York Moors village.

THE MALLYAN SPOUT HOTEL is set in spectacular countryside. While technically being a hotel, the bar area is a traditional pub in both décor and spirit. The beer garden is also a great spot for an alfresco lunch or post-walk drink.
☎ 01947 896486 ⊕ www.mallyanspout.co.uk

BIRCH HALL INN in Beck Hole makes a good refreshment stop around ¾ of the way along the route. ☎ 01947 896245
⊕ www.facebook.com/p/Birch-Hall-Inn-Beckhole

The Walk

① From the front of the **Mallyan Spout Hotel**, head along the path that runs between the hotel and the neighbouring café in the direction of the back of the hotel. In around ¼ mile on a narrow path heading gently downhill you will reach the river. At the river and signpost, turn left for another 100m, clambering over boulders and rocks to reach the waterfall.

② Carry on past the waterfall, crossing three bridges to reach a stile. Head up some steps, but importantly not up the 2nd set of steps. Continue instead to follow the river through ferns on a narrow riverside path. Carry on for what is just over ½ mile, hugging the riverside and clambering over rocks, boulders and through ferns until you meet a road at a stone bridge. Go carefully if the rocks are wet.

③ Turn left and follow the road for around 100m, turning right at a bridleway sign at the bend in the road. Take the next left in

Goathland 3

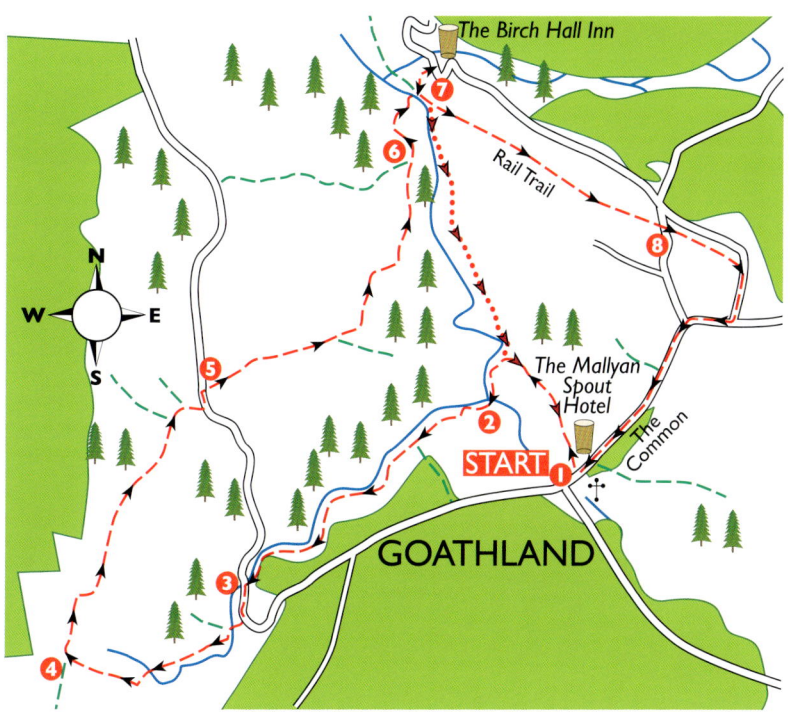

around 50m and cross the river on a metal and stone bridge. Walk uphill past a derelict house and through a succession of three gates. Carry on walking along the worn path skirting around the edge of the field uphill. All the time you are following **North York Moors Bridleway signs**. You then join a road at the top of the field where there is a stunning view across the valley.

④ Turn right along the road which in 200m bends to the right and then left heading downhill. Keep ahead on this farm road for around ½ mile, until you reach a main road beside farm buildings. Turn left and then in 50m take a right turn off the road, following a public footpath sign.

⑤ Keep left to follow the footpath signs across the fields heading downhill to woodland by a stile. The woodland is fairly dense but the path is clear. Carry on for ¼ mile passing through two gates.

6 Carry on descending and after another 100m take the path heading right to the river (not the bridleway straight on). After 50m downhill you reach steps down to two bridges over the river and then a signpost at **Beck Hole**. If you want to visit **Birch Hall Inn**, just 100m away, keep straight ahead and then retrace your steps back to the sign.

7 To continue the walk turn right at the signpost to head along the **Rail Trail** signposted to Goathland (left if you've been to the pub), and then after the houses there is another signpost. To shorten the walk by ½ mile turn right and follow the path for around ½ mile and then turn left to return to the hotel car park. Alternatively, keep ahead on the Rail Trail for ½ mile gradually heading uphill to reach the road.

8 Cross over the road to continue walking along the Rail Trail. Keep going for around 300m to reach another road. Turn right, following a sign for **Goathland Station**. At the T-junction turn right again to head through the village passing the gift and sweet shops, tearoom and general store. It's now ½ mile along the pavement through Goathland back to the **Mallyan Spout Hotel**.

Places of Interest Nearby

Soak up the atmosphere in Goathland by visiting the gift shop, tearoom and station. There is also the option to take a train on the **North Yorkshire Moors Railway** to another village or even the coast.

Walk 4

Kilburn & the White Horse

Distance: 4 miles (6.5 km)

Start: The Forresters Arms, The Square, Kilburn, YO61 4AH.

Parking: In the Square outside the Forresters Arms or roadside nearby.

OS Map: Explorer OL26 North York Moors, Western Area.
Grid Ref: SE513796.

Terrain: Involves a section of steep hillside steps, a couple of wooden step bridges and a 100m section of trickier terrain downhill. Otherwise mostly good terrain on road, field, or well-trodden forest tracks. Dog friendly.

Walk Tips: The last 1¼ miles of the route back from the wooden bridge onwards can be overgrown in summer. I would advise wearing trousers. Alternatively, you can merely carry on, not taking the right over the step bridge. This will take you back to the road, from where you can simply return to the village by the way you came. This route would also avoid the wooden step bridges and may therefore be easier for dogs.

This walk is at its best on a clear day, otherwise you'll miss out on the spectacular view from the top of the White Horse.

Kilburn & the White Horse ❹

Kilburn is a small, picturesque village with beautifully quaint cottages situated on the edge of the North York Moors National Park. This route takes you through the village and out into the surrounding woodland, towards the famous White Horse landmark sculpted into the hillside. The views from the hillside are truly unrivalled in the county, and the unique hillside artwork, dating from 1857, adds an extra flourish.

THE FORRESTERS ARMS is a modern and stylish gastro pub with accommodation above. They serve high quality restaurant-style food, while also catering for those who like traditional pub fare. The inn is situated in a central location on the main through-road of Kilburn, yet is in a tranquil village setting amongst many of the village's stone cottages.
☎ 01904 947570   🌐 www.forresterskilburn.co.uk

The Walk

❶ From the pub, turn right and head north along the road in the direction of the **White Horse**, passing many of the village's quaint cottages along the way. Pass a footpath sign on the left cutting through the hedge (which you will return through), a bench, and then a carved stone North York Moors sign as a view of the White Horse appears.

❷ After ½ mile, take the left fork signed White Horse, heading uphill. In another 100m take the path on the right which zigzags

North Yorkshire Pub Walks

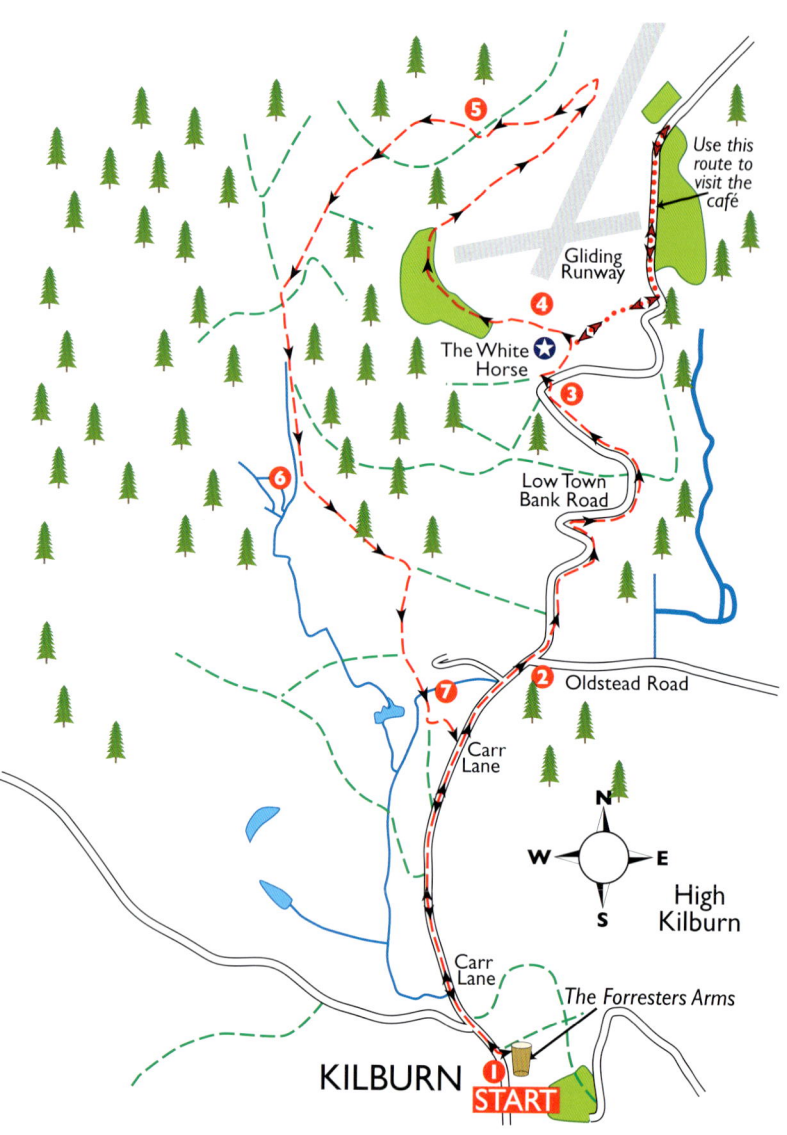

alongside the road uphill. Pass the first car park, before arriving at a second car park, at the bottom of the White Horse.

❸ From the car park information board, take the steps up to the

Kilburn & the White Horse

top of the hillside. It is less than 100m to the top but the steps and hillside are steep. At the top, the view is simply breathtaking. Carry on along the path to the left, across the top of the horse.

The White Horse artwork was created in 1857 by a local school master and his pupils, together with local volunteers. They exposed the underlying rock and then covered it with white limestone chippings. It is incredible that it has lasted, especially when considering that during World War II, the horse was covered over to prevent it from being used for navigation by enemy bombers.

4 You are now following the **Cleveland Way**. Keeping the gliding runway to your right, follow this path for just over ½ mile, before taking the first path on the left which drops down from the escarpment edge. Follow this steep downward path heading diagonally back on yourself.

5 Once at the bottom of the hill, the path flattens out, and joins another path coming in from the right. Just before this you need to head right and cross this other path to keep heading downhill on a bridleway. Continue heading downhill on the bridleway and in around ½ mile you will reach a wider forest track. Turn left here and then after around 200m, head down a narrower footpath forking off the forest track to the right.

North Yorkshire Pub Walks

6 The path bends around to the left towards a road. A few hundred metres before reaching the road, there are some wooden steps on your right climbing up and over a fence. Head over the wooden steps, and down towards a larger wooden bridge, somewhat grandly taking you over a field's entrance. The path then hugs the hedgerow (rather too closely in the height of summer) before you reach a gate into a field.

7 Skirt around the field to the right-hand side until you see another small wooden bridge heading over a stream. The path is then not clear but just head diagonally across the field (or around the left-hand side next to the road) until you see the gap in the hedge with a stile near the north end of Kilburn village which you walked past on the way out. At **Carr Lane** turn right and retrace your steps through the village to return to the pub.

Places of Interest Nearby

At the top of the hillside, just above the **White Horse**, is **Yorkshire Gliding Club**. This is one of the oldest gliding clubs in the world and is open to the public. You can take a look inside the control tower and there is a café inside. To get there, simply head east at the top of the steps by the White Horse and follow the path through woodland for a few hundred metres, before following the road to the airfield.

Walk 5

WHITBY & SANDSEND

Distance: 6¼ miles (10 km)

Start: Church Street Car Park, Church Street, Whitby, YO22 4AS.

Parking: Church Street Car Park. However, there are numerous car parks in Whitby within close proximity of the starting point.

OS Map: Explorer OL27 North York Moors, Eastern Area.
Grid Ref: NZ901109.

Terrain: Easy terrain throughout, being along pavement, promenade, grass or beach, with no hills. No dogs are allowed on the beach so if you want to make the route dog friendly you will need to retrace your steps along the clifftop back from Sandsend.

Walk Tips: Note that the leg along the beach cannot be done at high tide so please check tide times before you set off.

Walking along the road towards Sandsend offers great clifftop views, but could be avoided in part by joining the beach when you reach the golf course, which would avoid the busiest section of road.

Whitby is always an exciting place to visit, so make sure you allow some time to visit the numerous shops, or for taking on the 199-step ascent to the famous Whitby Abbey. This walk

North Yorkshire Pub Walks

starts from central Whitby and heads north along clifftops to the neighbouring but quieter village of Sandsend, where there is a traditional pub, the Hart Inn. The walk returns along the beach; three miles of continuous Yorkshire golden sand (or along the promenade). Just make sure you time the walk with the tide times.

THE HART INN in the village of Sandsend is a traditional cosy pub with a sophisticated and modern menu. Given the location it's no surprise to find plenty of seafood on offer. On a fine day, be sure to head out to the spacious and busy beer garden at the rear, complete with a wooden bar shack.
☎ 01947 893304   ⊕ www.thehartinn-sandsend.foodndrink.uk

THE MAGPIE CAFÉ, passed on the walk, is known throughout North Yorkshire as one of the best fish and chips restaurants around. A reputation that means there is usually a queue outside in all weathers!   ⊕ www.magpiecafe.co.uk

The Walk

❶ From **Church Street Car Park**, turn left to follow **Church Street** round to the left and across the **Swing Bridge** into the centre of **Whitby**. Turn right along **St Ann's Staith** to walk alongside the harbour, passing the fish market and the famous **Magpie Café**.

❷ After only a few minutes' walk, follow the road as it bends uphill, and after the seafood restaurant on the right and café on the left, take the steps dug into the cliff, by a blue signpost, heading in the direction of the **Captain Cook Memorial statue**. *At the top, turn around for the spectacular view of the Abbey through the famous Whale Bone Arch.* You are now going to follow the **Cleveland Way** all the way to the main road at **Whitby Golf Club**. Keep right to head through **Pavilion Drive Car Park**, passing the **Pavilion Theatre**, before following the signed path along the clifftops.

Whitby & Sandsend   5

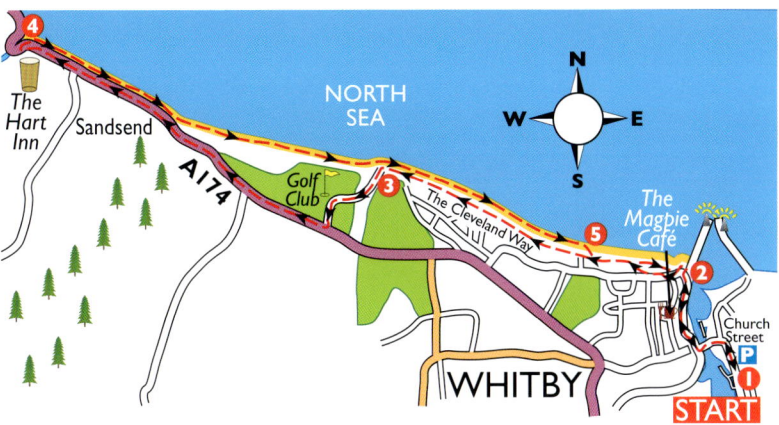

3 Follow the clifftop path until you reach **Whitby Golf Course** where the path bends inland. Keep following the path as it goes under a bridge and up to the main road (**Sandsend Road**). Turn right and walk along the pavement with sea views for roughly 1¼ miles, all the way to **Sandsend**.

North Yorkshire Pub Walks

4 As the road bends inland you'll find the **Hart Inn** just around the corner near the central bridge of Sandsend. For your return, retrace your steps to the beachside café and head down onto the beach. Simply walk along the beach back in the direction of Whitby, passing the **Pavilion Theatre**.

Rumour has it that Duleep Singh, the last Maharajah of the Sikh Empire, once took up residence in Mulgrave Castle, an estate near Sandsend, and used to do this journey along the beach from Sandsend to Whitby on elephants.

5 When you reach the **Pavilion Theatre** again, head up the slip road and keep ahead into the car park. Head up the steps to your right and walk the short distance along the pavement back to the **Captain Cook Memorial** and **Whalebone Arch**. Head back down the cliff steps and walk along the road and over the swing bridge to return to the car park.

Places of Interest Nearby

Wander through the spectacular gothic ruins of **Whitby Abbey** which inspired Bram Stoker's *Dracula*. The museum is also worth a visit where you can learn more about the history of the town and abbey and see Anglo-Saxon crosses along with medieval manuscripts. An alternative refreshment option in Sandsend would be to eat at the **Fish Cottage**, home to some of the best seafood on the Yorkshire coast.

Walk 6
Skipwith Common National Nature Reserve

Distance: 4½ miles (7 km)

Start: Skipwith Common Parking, King Rudding Lane, YO19 6QL.

Parking: Skipwith Common Parking.

OS Map: Explorer 290 York. **Grid Ref:** SE644373.

Terrain: Flat, hard trail paths and good terrain; perfect for a dog walk.

Walk Tips: If you plan to explore Skipwith Common further, either before or after the walk, I would advise taking a picture of the route map on the information board at the car park entrance, which will help you keep your bearings.

North Yorkshire Pub Walks

Skipwith Common is a designated Nature Reserve, containing over 700 acres of lowland heath, wetlands, ponds, reed-beds, woodland and scrubland. This ancient landscape is one of the best remaining areas of lowland heath in England. The walk takes you through the nature reserve, heads through Skipwith village to the Drovers Arms pub, then continues to loop around the edge and back through the nature reserve on your return.

THE DROVERS ARMS has a wide menu, ready for lunchtime walkers and fine diners alike. It is proud of its roaring fire, local ales, diverse selection of gins, and awards won - who wouldn't be!
☎ 01757 288088
🌐 www.thedroversarmsskipwith.com

The Walk

① From the back of the car park enter **Skipwith Common** and head straight ahead along the wide path in front of you. At the end of the path follow the yellow marker directing you straight on again. Keep following the yellow markers from here. If you

Skipwith Common National Nature Reserve 6

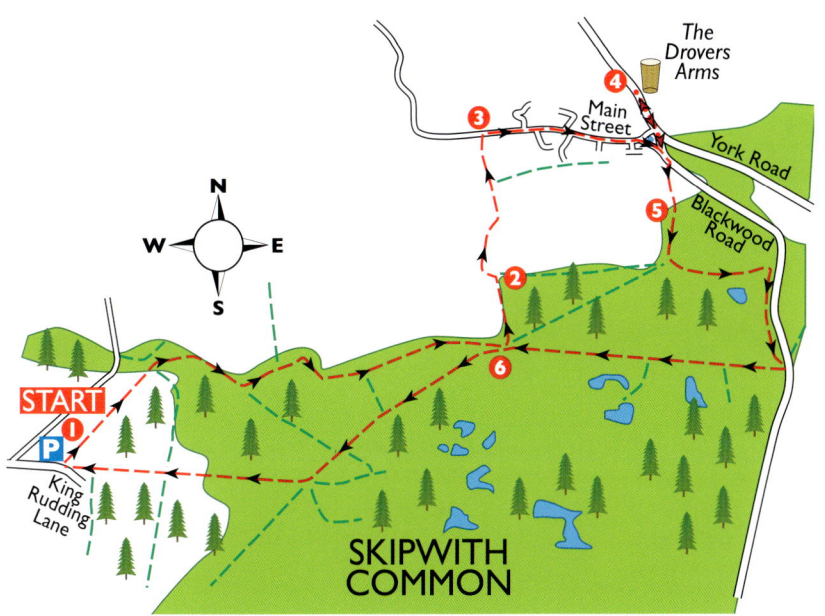

don't see one for a while, something has gone wrong so keep your eyes peeled. The place to pay the most attention is where there is a sign for **Sandy Lane Car Park** as you do not want to head for this, but instead turn left and continue on the yellow and blue signposted path.

❷ At the end of the 100m straight from the **Sandy Lane marker**, make sure to turn left following the yellow route out of the Common through a gate (and not the blue route). You then continue on the yellow path weaving through fields. The path heads in the direction of the church, which you get a good view of across the paddock. Eventually you come to the main road into Skipwith.

❸ Turn right along the road (**Main Street**) and continue walking along the pavement to the central village pond. If you wish to visit the **Drovers Arms**, bear left and then left again onto **York Road** and the pub is 50m further on. If you don't wish to visit the pub keep to the right of the pond and then take the first right down **Common Road** and jump to point 5.

4 After visiting the pub, return to the pond and this time carry on straight down **York Road** keeping the pond on your right, before peeling off to the right down Common Road.

5 Follow **Common Road** over a cattle grid to return to the nature reserve. Almost straightaway after entering the Common there is another yellow route marker on the left. Continue to follow the yellow markers again. The route heads to **Sandy Lane Car Park** where you turn right and follow the path straight ahead for ½ mile back to the centre point where you saw the original Sandy Lane Car Park sign. Follow the sign for **King Rudding Lane Car Park**.

6 Just 50m after the signpost, take the wider path heading diagonally left. When you reach the '**Bomb Bay Loop**', keep to the right-hand path, heading back to the car park.

Places of Interest Nearby

The nearby **Yorkshire Air Museum** in **Elvington** is one of the best attractions in the region. Here you can see everything from the oldest Cayley glider and Wright Flyer replicas from the 19th and early 20th century, to modern Tornado Jets. There are around 50 aircraft, many of which are kept in working condition and started up at certain events. Bonus point: dogs are allowed in the museum.

There is a gem of a café in the nearby village of **Wheldrake** called **Caffé Valeria**. Arriving here is like walking into the living room of a home… but in Sicily.

Walk 7
Danby Beacon

Distance: 6¾ miles (10.8 km)

Start: The Duke of Wellington, West Lane, Danby, YO21 2LY.

Parking: Lay-by parking on Briar Hill in the centre of Danby, 100m east of the Duke of Wellington pub.

OS Map: Explorer OL27 North York Moors, Eastern Area.
Grid Ref: NZ708086.

Terrain: Mostly tarmac country road and stone paths, with intermittent grass sections that can be muddy in wet weather. Dog friendly.

Walk Tips: This walk is at its best on a clear day; the focal point is Danby Beacon, from where there are spectacular 360-degree views over the surrounding countryside and coastline.

Danby is a wonderful village to visit, enveloped by spectacular countryside and offering plenty to do. The National Park Centre, known as Danby Lodge, gives a unique perspective from which to enjoy the North York Moors countryside, while Danby Beacon offers far-reaching views of the surrounding moors and Yorkshire coast. This walk takes in the Beacon, the National Park Centre, and the local countryside where there are further opportunities for truly stunning views.

North Yorkshire Pub Walks

THE DUKE OF WELLINGTON in Danby is an attractive 18th-century inn overlooking the village green. It served as a recruiting post for local regiments during the Napoleonic War, hence the name and the iron plaque of the Duke himself, which now sits above the open fire in the cosy bar. The traditional British menu, much of which is sourced locally, is only served in the evenings but this is still a great spot for a drink if the timings don't suit for a meal. Dogs are welcome in the main bar.

☎ 01287 660351   ⊕ www.dukeofwellingtondanby.co.uk

THE FOX & HOUNDS, tucked away in the neighbouring village of Ainthorpe, is the very definition of hidden gem. This dog-friendly country pub has a traditional feel complete with tartan carpet and log fire, and an extensive menu.
☎ 01287 660218   ⊕ www.foxandhoundsainthorpe.com

The Walk

❶ From the **Duke of Wellington** pub, cross the road and head along the road opposite the pub in the direction of Castleton. After 160m follow the footpath sign forking off right uphill on grass to **Hollin Farm**. Head through the farm, and then follow the vehicle tracks across the field. At the next gate and dry-stone wall, go right and along the wall for 100m before going through a gate to the right by a bridleway sign. You'll see the next gate 50m ahead taking you into a small woodland and downhill to a river and three stepping stones.

❷ After the river, there's a wooden bridge and a gate into a spinney. Head through the next gate and across the cottage's drive. Keep your eyes peeled for bridleway-marked wooden posts directing you uphill. After 60m uphill, join a clearer, wider path where you turn right towards the road (**West Lane**).

❸ Cross over the road and follow the signed bridleway opposite, which runs perpendicular to the road. The path bends right

Danby Beacon 7

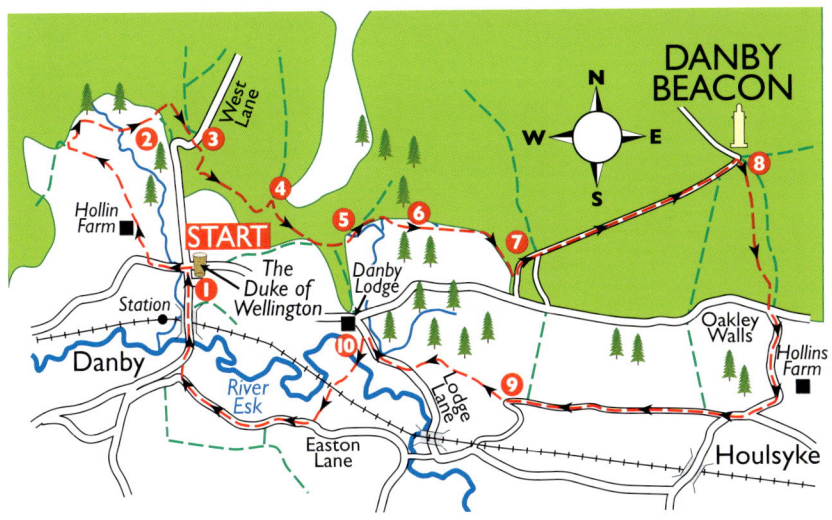

downhill to another cottage and then to a wide path where you turn left across the hillside, heading east and uphill. The view to the right here is spectacular.

4 As the path bends left (north), just before reaching the dry-stone wall, turn right along the grass path to continue eastwards. You will shortly see the road climbing uphill towards **Danby Beacon** ahead of you. At this point, it doesn't matter which path you follow across the hillside (there are a few criss-crossing), just head east, towards the wall at the southern, downhill end of the field.

5 In the bottom corner of the field, head through the gate and straight on downhill, through a gate into woodland. After the woodland, head diagonally downhill towards a stile and gap in the dry-stone wall at the river where you cross a bridge. Head diagonally uphill, slightly back on yourself, following a very faint path through ferns.

6 Follow the dry-stone wall uphill in the rocky field where there isn't a clear path and navigation around boulders is needed. Keep near the dry-stone wall and woodland on your right-hand side, and you'll eventually see a footpath marker post at the top of the hill.

North Yorkshire Pub Walks

7 Shortly after you bend round the dry-stone wall, head for a footpath post diagonally to your left uphill. You then reach the road around the 2½ miles mark and simply turn left uphill on the road for ¾ mile to reach the beacon. Here you will see a sweeping 360-degree view of the surrounding coast and countryside.

The Danby Beacon is one of a line of beacons up to 20 miles apart, dating back to the 1600s when the country was living under threat of invasion from France. The beacons would have been lit at the sight of a foreign fleet. During World War II, the site became home to one of the first radar stations guarding the north-east coast. It now has a flame-shaped metal basket, which is a link to the Bronze Age burial mound which once occupied the site.

8 Retrace your steps to the junction just before the beacon and head downhill for ½ mile on the stone path to the road (**Oakley Walls**). Cross straight over and through the gate to **Hollins Farm**, and then walk steeply downhill on the road into **Houlsyke**. When you meet the main road, turn right and after 20m head off

Danby Beacon 7

to the right onto the side road, walking uphill by the national speed limit signs.

9 After ½ mile, follow the **Esk Valley Walk** signpost and keep straight on through a farm. Head over the stile and across the top of the field, then follow the path diagonally across the field to the road (**Lodge Lane**). Turn right along the road to reach **Danby Lodge**. Diverting to the centre would add less than 200m to your walk and is well worth the detour.

10 In the Lodge's garden, there is a wooden bridge across the river (to the right of the front of the main building). Cross this and then go over the railway line to reach a road (**Easton Lane**). Turn right towards Ainthorpe and walk along the road for ½ mile before bearing right along a bridleway to cut off the road's corner. When you join the road again, turn right to head through Danby and back to your car.

Places of Interest Nearby

Danby Lodge National Park Centre is an excellent place to spend an hour or so; there is a café, a gallery that showcases revolving exhibitions throughout the seasons, a Yorkshire focused souvenir and gift shop, a manicured garden and walking trail. It is akin to a miniature museum, where you can find out about the places, geography and wildlife of the North York Moors.

Walk 8
Staveley Nature Reserve

Distance: 4¼ miles (7 km)

Start: Staveley Nature Reserve, Minskip Road, Staveley, HG5 9LQ.

Parking: Staveley Nature Reserve car park, off Minskip Road.

OS Map: Explorer 299 Ripon & Boroughbridge.
Grid Ref: SE369630.

Terrain: A flat, easy walk with good terrain throughout, except for a short section of farmland, which can be wet and boggy in winter. One stile. Dog friendly but dogs must be kept on a lead throughout the nature reserve.

Walk Tips: Staveley Nature Reserve is a venue for all weathers and conditions.

Staveley is not on the beaten track as far as tourist routes of North Yorkshire go, yet the village has an impressive wetland nature reserve, where over 200 species of bird have been seen. This walk loops around its lagoons on a lakeside trail, then explores some of the surrounding countryside and fields, before heading back through the nature reserve, passing the reserve's main bird hide and wildlife watching spot.

Staveley Nature Reserve 8

THE PUB

THE ROYAL OAK in Staveley is an attractive traditional pub situated in the heart of the village. The stone fireplace with log fire, tankards hanging from the ceiling and oak beams throughout, make it a cosy escape from the elements. Food is locally sourced and there is a good selection of local ales on offer. Dog friendly.

☎ 01423 340267   🌐 www.royaloakinnstaveley.co.uk

The Walk

1 From the nature reserve's car park, head through the gate by the information board and continue on the path, through a second gate a short distance ahead. At the first junction, take a right to head north towards **East Lagoon**.

2 At the next junction by the lagoon there is a bench and information board. Keep heading straight on down the left-hand side of the lagoon past the birdwatching hut. The path bends around the lagoon to the right and when you reach the bridge, head over it to leave the nature reserve by farm buildings.

3 Head straight on, following the right-hand path, towards the line of trees. The path initially goes between the trees and hedgerow and then follows the hedge down the side of a field. At the far side of the field, head straight on through the gate and past the barns on your left. As the lane bends to the right, head left to continue along the hedgerow towards a lonesome oak tree somewhat strangely positioned in the middle of the field.

4 From the oak tree, it's around ½ mile in a straight line through two metal gates to meet a track. Turn left past a house and head through another metal gate. Carry on straight for 300m ignoring any bridleway routes peeling off to the right, until

North Yorkshire Pub Walks

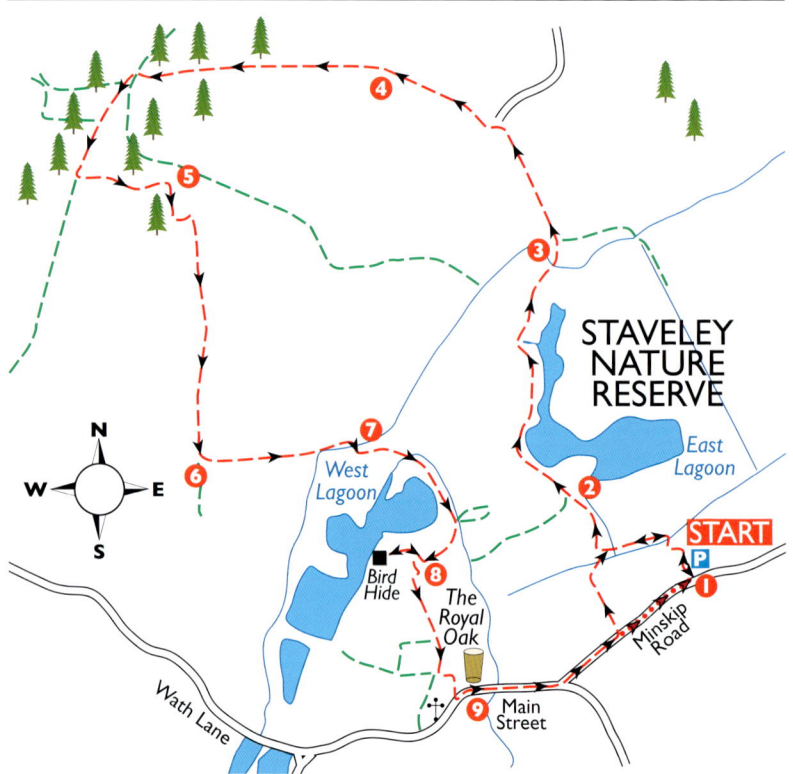

you see a stile and footpath sign leading into a field to the left. Follow the faint path across the field heading back towards **Staveley Nature Reserve**. Once you reach the brow of the hill in the field, you can see the footpath sign and stile straight ahead of you leading into the woodland.

5 Once through the trees, the path bends to the right between the edge of a field and the woodland. There is then a dog leg to the left then right, to continue along the border of the two fields. The path is not obvious along the short dog leg, but just cross the fence line where it is open within 20m of the woodland, before the hedge starts to the right. Once you are between the fields you should be on a grass bank separating the two fields heading in a westerly direction parallel with the nature reserve. The path along the grass bank between the two fields does become clearer. Walk along the edge of the field for around ½ mile towards the farm buildings.

Staveley Nature Reserve 8

6 Just before you reach the metal framed barns, at the junction at the end of the field, turn left to head in the direction of the nature reserve and along the other edge of the field. The path along this field is again not clear, but just keep heading towards the nature reserve along the field edge.

7 After ¼ mile the reserve's main wildlife and birdwatching hide at **West Lagoon** comes into view. In a further 100m you reach a bridge across a stream on the right which you cross to enter the nature reserve again. Turn left and follow the path for 200m to a junction where you bear right to walk alongside **West Lagoon**. After 100m go through a gate, and turn right to detour for 50m to the large hide.

8 Retrace your steps the 50m to the gate and continue along the path to the right. The path bends to the left and then heads towards the church in the village. After around 250m there is a junction of paths crossing the main country lane you're on. Take the alleyway to the left to cut through a residential garden which brings you out at the back of the **Royal Oak's car park**.

9 From the pub, turn left along the main road through the village. After 250m take the left fork, signed Minskip. After a few hundred metres, keep your eyes peeled for a signpost directing you left, down the side of houses and back into the nature reserve. This is a short detour to avoid walking the remaining 200m along a stretch of main road, but you can just continue along the road to return to your car. If taking the detour, once back in the nature reserve you will join the path you travelled out on. Turn right here and follow the path back to the car park.

Places of Interest Nearby

Yolk Farm near Minskip is well worth a visit. There is an impressively stocked luxury farm shop, and also a restaurant with a particular focus on dishes containing their free-range eggs. Chickens are obviously a big feature, but there are pigs and alpacas to meet too.

Walk 9

NEWTON UNDER ROSEBERRY & ROSEBERRY TOPPING

Distance: 6½ miles (10.5 km)

Start: Gribdale Gate Car Park, Dikes Lane, TS9 6HN.

Parking: Gribdale Gate – Captain Cook's Car Park, just off Dikes Lane. If you want to visit the pub before/after your walk park at the King's Head Inn and start the walk from point 6.

OS Map: Explorer OL26 North York Moors, Western Area.
Grid Ref: NZ592110.

Terrain: Mostly hard stone paths and good terrain, except for one descent of around ½ mile from Captain Cook's Monument, with awkward tree roots underfoot. There is also a considerable amount of hill climbing, with Roseberry Topping being a steep climb. Dog friendly.

Walk Tips: Roseberry Topping is perfectly positioned at the edge of the hillside for a sweeping view of Teesside on the flat plain below. The view from the top is truly spectacular, so do try to visit on a clear enough day to take in such an appropriate reward for the steep climb up to the top.

Newton under Roseberry & Roseberry Topping 9

This walk takes in some of North Yorkshire's best views and one of its finest natural features; Roseberry Topping. Colloquially known as the Yorkshire Matterhorn, at just over 320 metres, it isn't a particularly long climb, yet it towers over the surrounding countryside. Captain Cook's Monument is one of the few places in the county that could rival its view, and this is also explored within the first ½ mile of the walk. When combined with a halfway stop in the King's Head Inn, this route has to be one of the best pub walks in this (or any) county.

THE PUB

THE KING'S HEAD INN is a large, modern gastro pub surrounded by peaceful countryside. It lies in the shadow of Roseberry Topping, only ¼ mile from its base. The pub has earned a particular reputation for its Sunday roast, but the extensive menu means there is something to please all. The pub is also renowned for its dog friendliness. ☎ 01642 722318

🌐 www.inncollectiongroup.com/kings-head-inn

The Walk

❶ From the car park, turn left, heading west through the gate into **Gribdale Gate**, following the **Cleveland Way** signed to Kildale. Follow the path gradually uphill for ½ mile towards **Captain Cook's Monument**. At ½ mile there is a small monument to an RAF plane crash in 1940 where two people died.

You will need some time to take in the spectacular 360-degree view. The monument is so named in memory of Captain Cook who lived in Great Ayton nearby as a young boy. It is situated over 1000ft above sea level, offering a spectacular view over the landscape. You can also spot Roseberry Topping on the horizon.

❷ When you're ready, take the path opposite the plaque on the monument, heading north, and then bear right at the edge of the hilltop to walk along the edge of the hill and through two stone

North Yorkshire Pub Walks

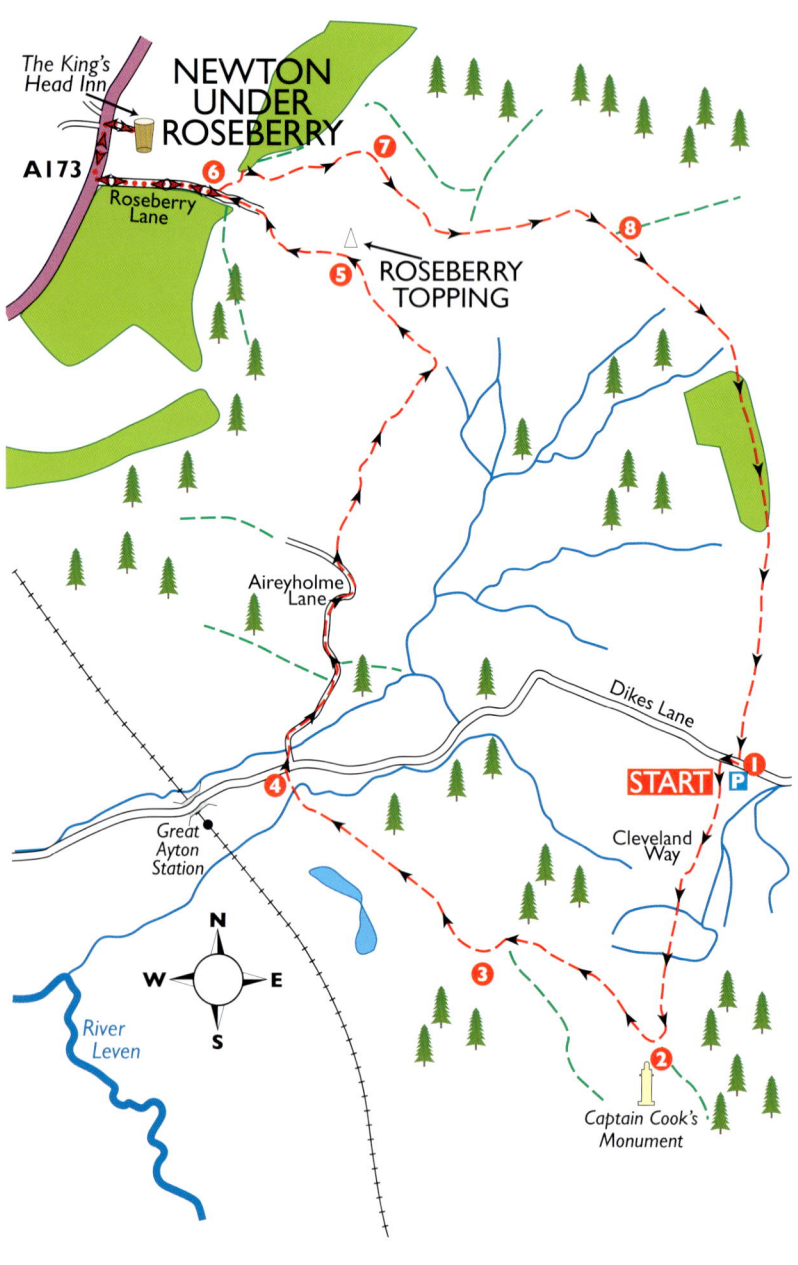

Newton under Roseberry & Roseberry Topping   9

pillars and a gap in the dry-stone wall. After 200m when the path forks, keep left heading downhill amongst the ferns. Keep going steeply downhill through woodland for ¼ mile to a dry-stone wall and continue following the footpath ahead and then round to the left, before taking a right onto a bridleway.

3 The route follows a dry-stone wall and offers amazing views to the left as well as of Roseberry Topping ahead. The terrain is rough here, with a lot of tree roots in the woodland so take care. Go through a gate, sticking to the bridleway as it becomes a lane and ignoring a path off to the left. Keep ahead and in ½ mile you'll reach a road at a junction by a couple of white houses.

4 Cross over the road to head up **Aireyholme Lane**. In ½ mile you will reach a farm. Go through a gate and turn right heading directly for Roseberry Topping. After 300m keep ahead through a gate onto a bridleway. After another gate the path meets a track where you turn left heading directly uphill. You can see the next gate ahead of you further uphill. Here you meet steep steps heading up to the top of Roseberry Topping, where there is a stone cairn to mark your achievement, along with spectacular 360-degree views again.

Roseberry Topping's famous pointed Matterhorn-style outline was caused by a landslip in 1912, prior to which it looked more akin to a volcano.

5 From the summit, continue in the direction you travelled up, heading down the other side, taking another set of steep steps. Continue on this path downhill, to a gate where you join **Roseberry Lane**. If visiting the pub, follow the lane to a road

North Yorkshire Pub Walks

where you turn right to reach the **King's Head Inn**, and then return to the gate at the end of **Roseberry Lane** to continue the walk.

6 If you do not wish to visit the pub, turn right at the gate by **Roseberry Lane** (left if you're coming from the direction of the pub). After 100m go through a gate straight ahead and then another to the right, heading into an area designated as **Roseberry Topping National Trust**. Follow the steps uphill for 50m then bear left on the stone path to head through a gate. You're then walking on a path through ferns.

7 Climb gradually uphill, skirting around the hillside with Roseberry Topping to your right. After ½ mile some paths criss-cross your path but just keep heading along this main path to reach a wall and gate. Don't go through the gate but head left towards a solitary tree and start climbing **Little Roseberry Hill** on a stone path. As the stone steps swing right, you head left to summit **Little Roseberry** to get a good view of Roseberry Topping.

8 Return to the stone path, and carry on up to the gate and bench ahead. Go through the gate, and then take the right-hand path alongside the dry-stone wall. Continue along this path for 1¼ miles back to your car.

Places of Interest Nearby

The nearby village of **Great Ayton** is worthy of a visit in its own right. With a half-mile long high street and a central hub of shops and cafés there's plenty to see and do. Don't miss the **Captain Cook Schoolroom Museum** (where the man himself received his early education) which is packed with displays about his early life.

Walk 10
ROSEDALE ABBEY

Distance: 4 miles (6.5 km)

Start: White Horse Farm Inn, Gill Lane, Rosedale Abbey, YO18 8SE.

Parking: White Horse Farm Inn car park on Gill Lane, just off Daleside Road, but please ask the landlords permission.

OS Map: Explorer OL26 North York Moors, Western Area.
Grid Ref: SE724954.

Terrain: Mostly hard stone paths and country lane walking. The first ½ mile is mostly uphill, with some steep sections, but relatively flat after this point. Dog friendly.

Walk Tips: Expect spectacular views on your route across the moors to Rosedale Abbey, around Chimney Bank, and from your pub table, with White Horse Farm Inn's benches being perfectly placed for an alfresco lunch.

Rosedale Abbey is one of the most impressive villages in North Yorkshire. It was a hive of activity in the 19th and early 20th century, when magnetic ironstone was discovered locally and the village's population grew from 500 to 3,000 within 20 years. However, since the closing of the mines in the 1920s, it has become somewhat more sedate. The fact that many industrial ruins still remain, combined with the village's spectacular location in the Rosedale Valley, makes the area very popular with

North Yorkshire Pub Walks

walkers. This route starts at White Horse Farm Inn and heads up the side of Chimney Bank, claimed to be one of the steepest roads in the country, before looping through the top of the moors and returning to the inn.

THE PUB **WHITE HORSE FARM INN** is an award-winning, 16th-century hilltop inn where you'll find a menu of pub classics alongside daily specials including seasonal Yorkshire game. There is a cosy bar with a log fire for colder months and outside seating from which you can truly appreciate the surroundings. With the inn's benches positioned to take full advantage of the wonderful vista, there isn't likely to be a pub with a better view in the region.
☎ 01751 417239   🌐 www.whitehorserosedale.co.uk

The Walk

❶ From **White Horse Farm Inn** cross straight over the road and head towards the golf course. After 150m turn left through a gate and follow a path to your right, through the golf course to a gate taking you through a hedge. Turn left to reach another gate at the top of the short but steep field. Continue left on the path through ferns uphill and over a stile.

❷ After the stile, Rosedale's famous archways, **Bank Top Kilns**, come into view at the top of the hill. Keep heading uphill and to the right of the farmhouse. When you join the farmhouse's drive by the tree, keep right along the drive for 50m and then turn left at the top. The view of the surrounding countryside is simply stunning as you walk behind the farmhouse.

❸ Bear left on the narrower footpath level with the farmhouse, to walk in front of **Bank Top Kilns**.

These archways were once kilns used to roast (calcine) the mined ore with coal in order to get rid of impurities and therefore increase the percentage of iron before it was transported via the railway. The scenic

Rosedale Abbey 10

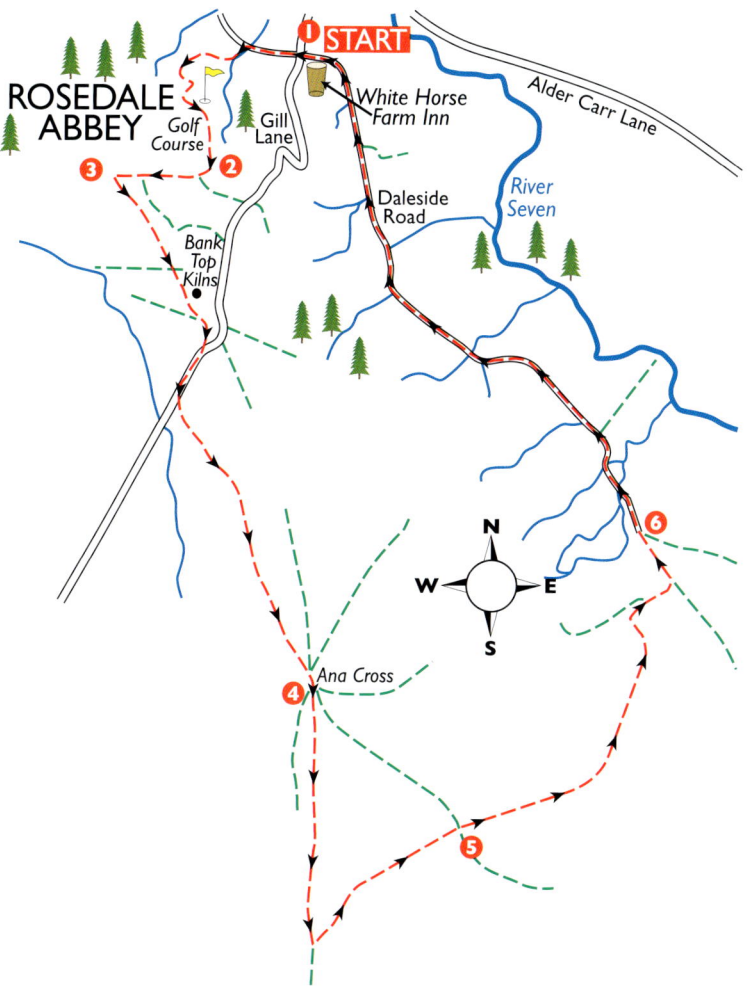

route of the railway can still be followed on foot in many places around Rosedale.

At the car park, turn right and head 50m up the road to the next car park. Turn left heading towards the concrete bunker. You will then see the track behind this structure which you join. In 100m the **Ana Cross** comes into view.

North Yorkshire Pub Walks

4 At the **Ana Cross**, carry on walking beyond it along the track through heather for another ¼ mile to a junction of paths. At the first junction after the cross, turn left almost back on yourself with the cross now visible again to your left.

5 When you meet another path coming from the cross to the left, cutting across the path you're on, head straight on, to follow the narrower path across the heather. You then bend to the left heading steeply downhill and then bear to the right. After 50m turn left joining another path heading downhill towards a solitary farm.

6 Follow the dry-stone wall downhill for 250m to a signpost and stone road at the farm. It is then a simple 1 mile back to the pub car park along this stone road with hillside views to your right.

Places of Interest Nearby

Not only is **Chimney Bank** one of the steepest roads in the country, but the views are truly spectacular. Even better, you can appreciate them from benches by the side of the road.

Hutton-le-Hole to the south west, is the closest village and is well worth a visit. It is a hive of activity and home to a pub, tea room, bakery, chocolate shop, **Ryedale Folk Museum** and more. See Walk 2 in this book for a walk starting from the village.

Paul Buckingham

Walk 11
NEWTON-ON-OUSE

Distance: 3¾ miles (6 km)

Start: The Dawnay Arms, Newton-on-Ouse, YO30 2BR.

Parking: Roadside on Cherry Tree Avenue or in the car park at the Dawnay Arms if visiting.

OS Map: Explorer 290 York. **Grid Ref:** SE511601.

Terrain: Field trails and riverside paths with no hills. Can be very wet underfoot and the River Ouse has been known to flood so the route is best undertaken during the drier months. Dog friendly.

Walk Tips: The River Ouse is notorious for flooding, so make sure you don't undertake this walk after a period of heavy rain, otherwise the riverside path could be impassable.

This walk starts in the village of Newton-on-Ouse, before skirting the estate of the National Trust's Beningbrough Hall. The house is in the Baroque style, but very little is known about its early history. It was requisitioned during World War II and used as a billet for aircrews stationed at RAF Linton-on-Ouse, before being handed over to the National Trust in 1958. There are good views of the house from much of the walk, and the last section heads back along the River Ouse to finish at the popular riverside pub, the Dawnay Arms.

North Yorkshire Pub Walks

THE PUB — **THE DAWNAY ARMS** is situated on the banks of the River Ouse and is highly regarded in the area (therefore it is advisable to book ahead, especially on a Sunday). The pub has a cosy bar area, complete with log fire, along with a more elaborate restaurant area. The outside dining area looks down over the pub lawns to the river bank. The food is rather fancier than your average small village pub, and priced accordingly, but it is still a firm favourite with locals and walkers.
☎ 01347 848345 ⊕ www.thedawnayatnewton.co.uk

THE PUB — **THE BLACKSMITHS ARMS** is almost directly opposite and is a traditional country pub with a nice beer garden to the front, making it a good alternative.
☎ 01347 848249 ⊕ www.facebook.com/blacksmithsnewton

The Walk

❶ From the **Dawnay Arms**, turn right along **Cherry Tree Avenue** towards the main gates of **Beningbrough Hall**. You will pass **All Saints' Church** on the right, with its 150ft spire which used to guide planes home to the nearby RAF Linton-on-Ouse during World War II.

❷ Once through the gates of **Beningbrough Hall** head left into woodland. (If the gates are closed, you can instead turn left

Newton-on-Ouse 11

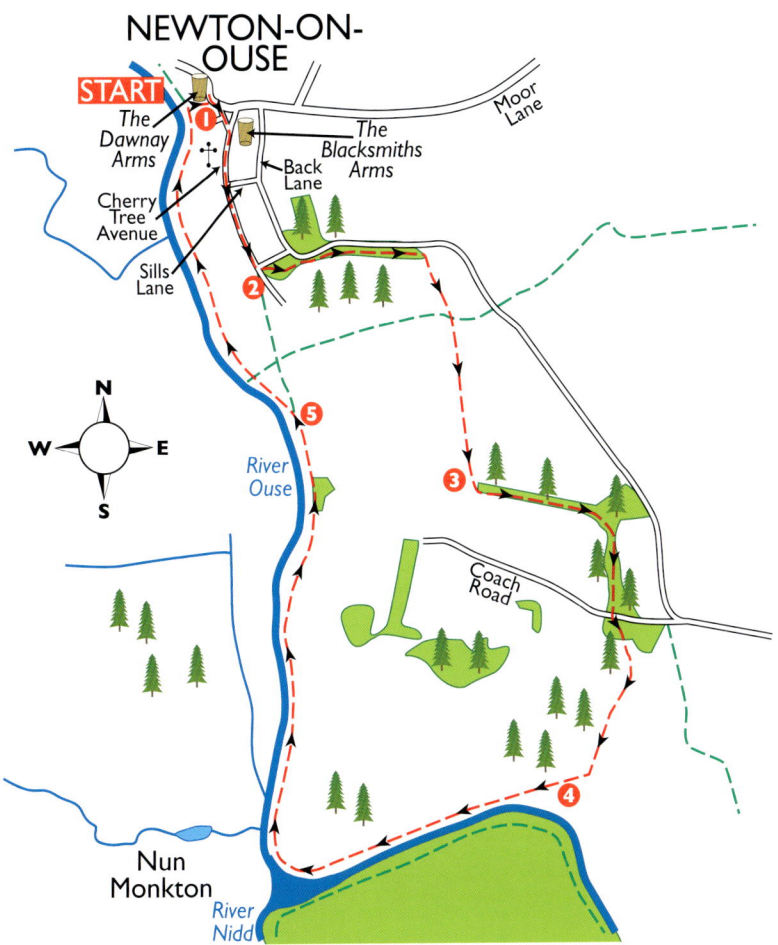

along **Sills Lane**, then right at the end of the road (**Back Lane**) to enter the woodland just after the left-hand bend in the road.) Follow the path weaving through the woodland, and then swing right as the path continues between fields. A beautiful view of Beningbrough Hall comes into sight beyond the trees and you'll pass a wooden frame, designed for you to take a picture of the hall through.

❸ In ¼ mile pass a couple of picnic benches and then turn left through woodland to continue skirting the boundary of the

estate. Follow the path as it bends to the right and then head through a gate to reach **Coach Road**. Cross the road and go through the metal gate opposite to follow the yellow National Trust walk sign.

4 At the end of the woodland there's a gate. Turn right here to follow the **River Ouse** as it runs along the edge of the estate. Follow the riverside path round to the right where the **River Nidd** joins the **River Ouse**. Across the river here is the village of Nun Monkton and its jetty. Carry on following the riverside path, past the now derelict **Nun Monkton Ferry Boat House**.

5 When you're back at the edge of the estate near Newton-on-Ouse, instead of heading towards Beningbrough's gates again, bear left at the fork sticking to the riverside path which runs along the back gardens of the houses on **Cherry Tree Avenue**. This is a fascinating section of the walk, and at times you will be convinced that you must have gone the wrong way and you're trespassing in someone's garden; however, there is a right of way footpath. In ½ mile you'll reach the **Dawnay Arms**'s gardens, where you turn right to return to your car.

Places of Interest Nearby

A pitstop at **Linton Lock**, in the neighbouring village of **Linton-on-Ouse**, is definitely recommended. There's a pretty weir and the **Lockhouse Café** situated in an old stone cottage at the side of the working lock. Take a minute to sit on one of the wooden benches and watch the boats come and go.

Walk 12

Malham

Distance: 5 miles (8 km)

Start: Malham National Park Centre, Chapel Gate, Malham, BD23 4DA.

Parking: Yorkshire Dales National Park Car Park, behind the visitor centre.

OS Map: Explorer OL2 Yorkshire Dales – Southern & Western Areas. **Grid Ref:** SD899627.

Terrain: Mostly stone and hard paths with a short woodland trail section and some field walking. Dog friendly, but caution is needed at the top of the Cove, due to the precarious terrain and cliff edge.

Walk Tips: This is a premier outdoors spot, with lots to see and do. I would advise you undertake this walk when you have a full day to explore some of the village's other attractions, including Malham Tarn and Beck Hall.

Malham is one of the main visitor destinations in the Yorkshire Dales, being locally famous for its spectacular natural attractions and beautiful countryside; there are limestone cliffs, crags, scars, woodland, some of the finest country views, miles of ancient dry-stone walls and an abundance of wildlife throughout, with

North Yorkshire Pub Walks

much of the dramatic scenery being designated as a Site of Special Scientific Interest. This walk takes in some of Malham's finest beauty spots, including Janet's Foss waterfall, the gorge of Gordale Scar, as well as a visit to the top and bottom of the famous Malham Cove.

THE PUB **THE LISTER ARMS** is in a central, picturesque part of Malham village and has all that you would want from a walkers' pub; flagstone floors, open fires and an extensive menu. They aim to serve hearty Yorkshire meals in welcoming surroundings, and they seem to succeed in that. It is therefore busy with muddy boots and dogs throughout the seasons.
☎ 01729 830444   ⊕ www.listerarms.co.uk

THE PUB Alternatively, try **BECK HALL**, arguably one of *the* culinary destinations in North Yorkshire. Accessed by walking over a very narrow stone bridge across the river, it is an almost magical approach to the wrap-around garden surrounding the restaurant and hotel; a wonderfully tranquil spot for a post-walk lunch or a summer's drink.
☎ 01729 830729   ⊕ www.beckhallmalham.com

The Walk

1 From the **Visitor Centre**, turn left into **Malham** and take the second footpath on the right after 100m, signposted Janet's Foss and Gordale Scar. Head over **Malham Beck** on a small stone

Malham 12

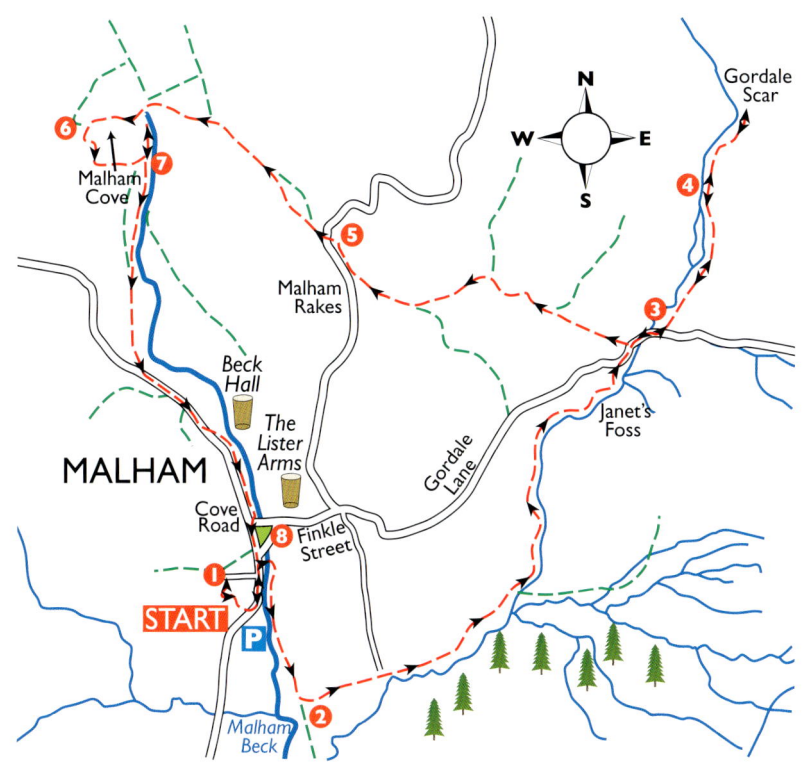

bridge and then turn right. Go through a gate and follow the river downstream.

2 A series of gates follow as you arc to the left by a stone barn. Continue on the path for another mile as it follows the river through more gates until you enter the National Trust area and **Janet's Foss waterfall**.

3 Pass to the left of the waterfall heading uphill and out to meet a road where a signpost sends you to the right towards **Gordale Scar**. After 50m, head over a stone bridge where there is a signpost to your left heading to **Malham Cove**. This is the path you will take after a short detour to see **Gordale Scar**. Keep ahead on the road and in a further 50m turn left at the sign to Gordale Scar, which takes you through a field.

④ As you continue on the path you head further into the natural valley. When the path swings to the right you suddenly get a great view of the gorge and waterfall. After visiting the scar, retrace the ½ mile to the stone bridge to take the signed path to the right towards **Malham Cove**. The path follows a dry-stone wall uphill to a series of gates before heading left and hugging the hillside as the view opens up and Malham is hidden below you amongst the trees.

⑤ You reach the road (**Malham Rakes**) at 3 miles. Cross over and then climb the wooden ladder over the dry-stone wall just to your right. After ¼ mile through the field a spectacular view of the Cove comes into sight. You then pass through a gate and head out onto the top of the Cove. It's around 200m to cross the Cove and can be slow going as you carefully make your way across the limestone, trying to avoid the chasms and cracks between the rocks. There are two views that are truly spectacular; one from the edge of the Cove down the valley to the river below, and another simply looking across the top of the limestone.

⑥ Once on the other side of the limestone, head for the path down to the valley floor, following steep stone steps. At the bottom the path forks; divert left for 150m upstream and towards the Cove for yet another spectacular view.

⑦ Retrace your steps to the fork and keep following the river path. Follow the path for ½ mile along the valley floor back to Malham.

Malham 12

The path joins **Cove Road** where you keep ahead through the village. Just after **Beck Hall** there's a signpost to the left directing you into woodland which avoids walking along the road. At the gate at the end of the woodland, the **Lister Arms** is 50m to the left over the small stone bridge and river.

8 To return to your car, turn left when you reach **Cove Road**, passing the **Buck Inn** and the **Old Barn Tearoom** and in 200m you will reach the **Malham National Park Centre** and car park.

Places of Interest Nearby

Malham Tarn, owned by the National Trust, is one of only eight upland alkaline lakes in Europe and is also the largest natural lake in North Yorkshire. The Tarn is not just important to wildlife, but is also one of the sources of the River Aire. From the top of Malham Cove, you could walk to the lake (1½ miles away) but I would instead suggest driving to the lake's car park after your walk, as this enables you to do a more comprehensive walking loop of the tarn, which could be anything up to 4½ miles in distance.

Walk 13
CRAYKE

Distance: 3 miles (4.5 km)

Start: The Durham Ox, West Way, Crayke, YO61 4TE.

Parking: The Durham Ox car park or roadside on Church Hill, opposite the pub.

OS Map: Explorer 299 Ripon & Boroughbridge.
Grid Ref: SE561705.

Terrain: Good terrain throughout; mostly worn field paths and only one small hill to climb. Dog friendly.

Walk Tips: There is the option to include a visit to the small Bakehouse Yorkshire café on the route at point 4.

Crayke is a quaint, peaceful village on a hilltop overlooking the Vale of York. The village retains its historic charm to this day, with an array of old stone cottages lining both sides of the main street. This walk loops around Crayke through fields and woodland, before returning to the top of the village by the church and now privately owned 15th-century castle. The route culminates with a beautiful landscape view before a stop at one of the finest pubs in the vicinity.

Crayke 13

THE DURHAM OX dates back 300 years and is now an award-winning inn, regularly featuring in *The Good Pub Guide*. The pub retains its authentic country inn style, with flagstone floors, exposed wooden beams and open fires. The menu contains plenty of pub classics along with a lighter lunchtime selection of sandwiches. Ingredients are sourced locally wherever possible. A section of the pub is dog friendly, but booking is advised as these tables are limited.

☎ 01347 821506   🌐 www.thedurhamox.com

The Walk

1 With your back to the **Durham Ox**, turn right and head down the hill towards Brandsby. After 250m, opposite **Mill Lane**, turn right along the single track lane between houses.

2 After ¼ mile you reach a field, where you turn left to head along the field edge. Carry on straight ahead, keeping to the field edge, through a dog leg following numerous small stones with mosaics on, until you reach a tarmac drive, which you follow to your right.

3 After 50m keep left along a grassy path, leaving the drive as it bends to the right towards the farmhouse. Enter woodland and then after 50m take the path on your right. Follow the track as it weaves through the wood, over the **River Foss** and into a field. The path continues left across the field alongside the river to a gate.

North Yorkshire Pub Walks

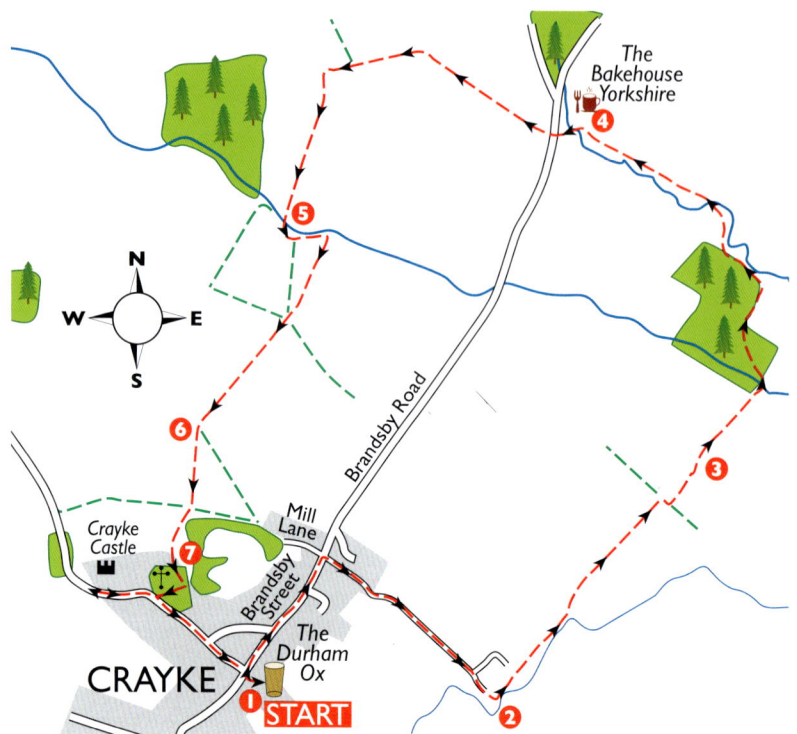

4 Head into the private garden of **Crayke Plant Nursery** (now closed but where there is still a permissive footpath). Head over the wooden bridge on your left and up to the road. Cross over the road and through the metal gate on the other side. Follow the path between hedgerows as it then bends round to the left. Turn left at the footpath sign directing you along the side of a field by an oak tree. You can now see **Crayke Castle** on the hilltop in front of you.

5 At the end of the field cross a wooden bridge. Turn left here following the sign, keeping to the field edge as it takes you uphill past a bench and across a farm track with farm buildings to your left.

6 Keep ahead to reach a way-marker at the end of the field which directs you through a gateway and diagonally across the next

Crayke

field, taking the steeper, faint grass path on your right-hand side, heading uphill towards a log seat and gate at the back of the churchyard.

7 Head through the churchyard, passing the front of the church and down the steps at the far right-hand side. The **Durham Ox** and your car are just down the road to your left, but it is worth the 150m diversion to the right to see **Crayke Castle**. Head for the bench on the left just past the gates to the castle, for an amazing view over the Vale of York. Afterwards, retrace your steps to the church steps and head along **Church Hill** to the **Durham Ox**.

Places of Interest Nearby
Crayke is on the edge of the Howardian Hills and close to many of North Yorkshire's finest villages. The attractive market town of **Easingwold** (around two miles to the east) is a must for anyone who likes independent shops and cafés.

Walk 14
Byland Abbey & Mount Snever Observatory

Distance: 3½ or 4 miles (5.5 or 6.5 km)

Start: The Abbey Inn, Byland Abbey, YO61 4BD.

Parking: There is a small car park opposite the Abbey or if visiting the Abbey Inn, use the car park behind the pub.

OS Map: Explorer OL26 North York Moors – Western Area.
Grid Ref: SE548789.

Terrain: Mostly good terrain on forest trails and field paths, except for a 100m section of rough terrain downhill after the observatory. There is quite a lot of uphill walking for much of the first part of the route. Dog friendly.

Walk Tips: The walk can also start and end at the Stapylton Arms in Wass, which would shorten the route by around ½ mile. Head along Hambleton Lane opposite the pub car park (by a bench and village notices) and start the walk from point 2.

The crumbling remains of Byland Abbey are nothing short of spectacular. So close to the passing road, yet nestled beautifully in quiet countryside on the edge of the Howardian Hills, the

Byland Abbey & Mount Snever Observatory 14

former monastery makes for an impressive yet unexpected sight. This walk also holds another surprise; the route takes you uphill through fields, quiet tracks, and forest for the best part of two miles to the top of Mount Snever, where you'll find a derelict and slightly spooky observatory, occupying a small clearing of forest on the hilltop. Also known as Oldstead Tower, it was completed in 1838 by John Wormald, the son of the Lord Mayor of York to celebrate the accession to the throne of Queen Victoria.

THE ABBEY INN is one of only a few pubs that could truly live up to these surroundings. A renovation in 2023 by celebrity Yorkshire chef Tommy Banks put the establishment on the map in North Yorkshire after being a traditional tearoom previously. As you might expect, they serve high quality food, specialising in locally sourced ingredients, much of which is grown on the owner's farm in the neighbouring village of Oldstead. They like to make use of foraged herbs to enhance their menus – ice cream flavoured with sweet cicely isn't out of place here. ☎ 01347 868204 ⊕ www.abbeyinnbyland.co.uk

THE STAPYLTON ARMS is situated in the neighbouring picturesque village of Wass. Here you'll find a traditional pub menu that can be enjoyed in the bar by the roaring fire or in the elegant restaurant.
☎ 01347 868280 ⊕ www.thestapylton.co.uk

The Walk

1 From the front of the pub and facing the **Abbey**, turn left on the road towards Wass. After 200m turn left into a farm driveway and then immediately right over the stile walking towards another stile and across the field beyond. Head diagonally uphill on the grass path, past a bench and through the gate in the corner of the field. Cross the next field, through the gate and out onto a lane (**Hambleton Lane**). Turn right here if you wish to visit the **Stapylton Arms** in **Wass** or left to continue the walk.

North Yorkshire Pub Walks

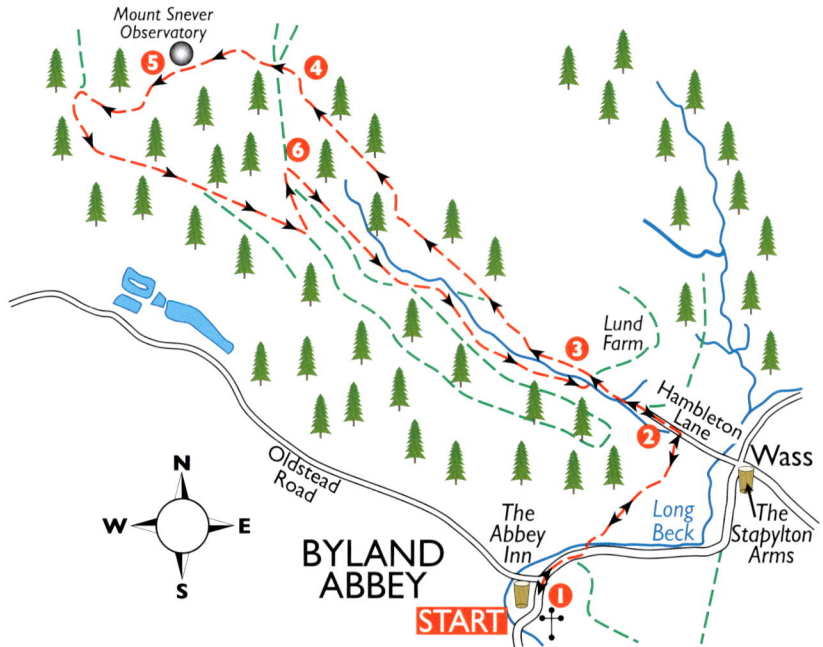

❷ Hambleton Lane soon becomes a wide track and starts to head uphill. Keep ahead ignoring a path to your right. Pass a sign for **Lund Farm** and at a right-hand bend, carry straight on through the pedestrian gate. The woodland is now on your left with ferns and hillside on your right. Follow the path along the edge of the trees and after 250m head for the cutting on your right through bushes. You will eventually meet a stile leading you into woodland.

❸ Bear right in the wood, not heading downhill. Then after 100m bear right again off the main woodland path onto a pedestrian path heading more steeply uphill.

❹ After ½ mile the view opens out into fields ahead. At the junction with a stile on your right, again head straight on, not over the stile or downhill to your left. Carry on keeping the stone wall to your right and in 100m, veer left towards the centre of the wood. **Mount Snever Observatory** will appear 20m in front of you, just as you are starting to doubt that there could possibly be an observatory anywhere near this point.

Byland Abbey & Mount Snever Observatory 14

Mount Snever Observatory is now derelict and has been for some time. However it is just as impressive as I'm sure it would have been when first built to commemorate the coronation of Queen Victoria.

5 After admiring the observatory, head steeply downhill from the front of it, on rough terrain and past a swamp on your left after 100m. After another 250m you come to a track with a signpost to **Oldstead**. Turn left and head along the woodland track. Carry on along this track, ignoring a fork off to the right. Follow the track as it bends left and in 200m, just after the footpath sign to Wass, take a right past the historic wreck of a tractor.

6 Follow the path as it descends steeply and 100m past another sign for Wass, take a right onto the more established track, not heading down into the dip and over the stream. After ¼ mile you will join the track opposite the entrance to **Lund Farm**. Turn right and retrace your steps back to the **Stapylton Arms** or the car park at **Byland Abbey**.

Places of Interest Nearby

Owned by English Heritage, **Byland Abbey** is free to enter, and the ruins are well worth a visit. It's not often you get the opportunity to see such an impressive structure at close quarters. An excellent example of early gothic architecture, it's said to have inspired the design of many other church buildings, including the rose window at York Minster. Don't miss the collection of medieval floor tiles that are still in situ to this day; remarkably this is the largest collection still existing in Europe. Note that the tiles are covered during the colder months for protection against the elements.

Walk 15
MASHAM

Distance: 6½ miles (10.5 km)

Start: King's Head Hotel, Market Square, Masham, HG4 4DZ.

Parking: Masham Square Car Parking, Chapman Lane in the centre of Masham.

OS Map: Explorer 302 Northallerton & Thirsk.
Grid Ref: SE225807.

Terrain: A mixture of country road, field and woodland walking. Hackfall wood has hills, undulations, steps, muddy sections and paths with exposed tree roots, and can occasionally be tricky underfoot. Six stiles towards the end of the walk may also make it unsuitable for some dogs.

Walk Tips: Hackfall wood is a wonderful place to explore for an hour. If you have the time to extend the length of the walk, I would recommend doing so. There are numerous twists and turns, great views and impressive follies along many different paths, weaving up and down the hillside. It's worth doing a bit of research before setting off and getting a map of the area.

Masham is a pretty and characterful town arranged around a Georgian market square. The town is famous for its breweries and regular town square farmers' markets and has a range of

Masham 15

local shops, tearooms and places to eat, making it a popular destination all year round. This walk starts at the market square and follows the river across fields to Hackfall, an evocative Victorian woodland with dramatic scenery and impressive follies, before returning to Masham through more woodland, across fields and along country roads.

THE PUB

THE KING'S HEAD HOTEL occupies a prominent position, on what is the largest market square in Yorkshire. The 18th-century Georgian inn has evolved with the historic town and is now a modern and busy gastropub with accommodation, and is part of the Chef & Brewer chain. The restaurant has a hotel feel to it and the food is somewhat more adventurous than your average pub. Dogs are more than welcome.
☎ 01765 689295 ⊕ www.chefandbrewer.com/pubs/north-yorkshire/kings-head/hotel

The Walk

❶ Facing the **King's Head Hotel** in **Market Square**, turn right and then turn left down **Chapman Lane**. At the junction with **Park Street** turn left, passing a large factory on your right. Cross a stone bridge and turn left immediately on the other side.

❷ Keeping the river to your left, head along the public footpath and across a succession of fields and wooden bridges. Head up some wooden steps in the field and continue to follow the river as it curves round to the right, passing the various **Swinton Estate fishing sites**, with somewhat mysterious names such as **Stony Pool**, and **Roman Pool**. Keep ahead through four gates to reach woodland.

❸ Enter the woodland to continue following the riverside path. Pass more fishing spots, including **Hackfall Pool** and **Deep Pond** and then head uphill away from the river, keeping left towards a stream. Cross the stream and then head through the gate into **Hackfall wood**.

71

North Yorkshire Pub Walks

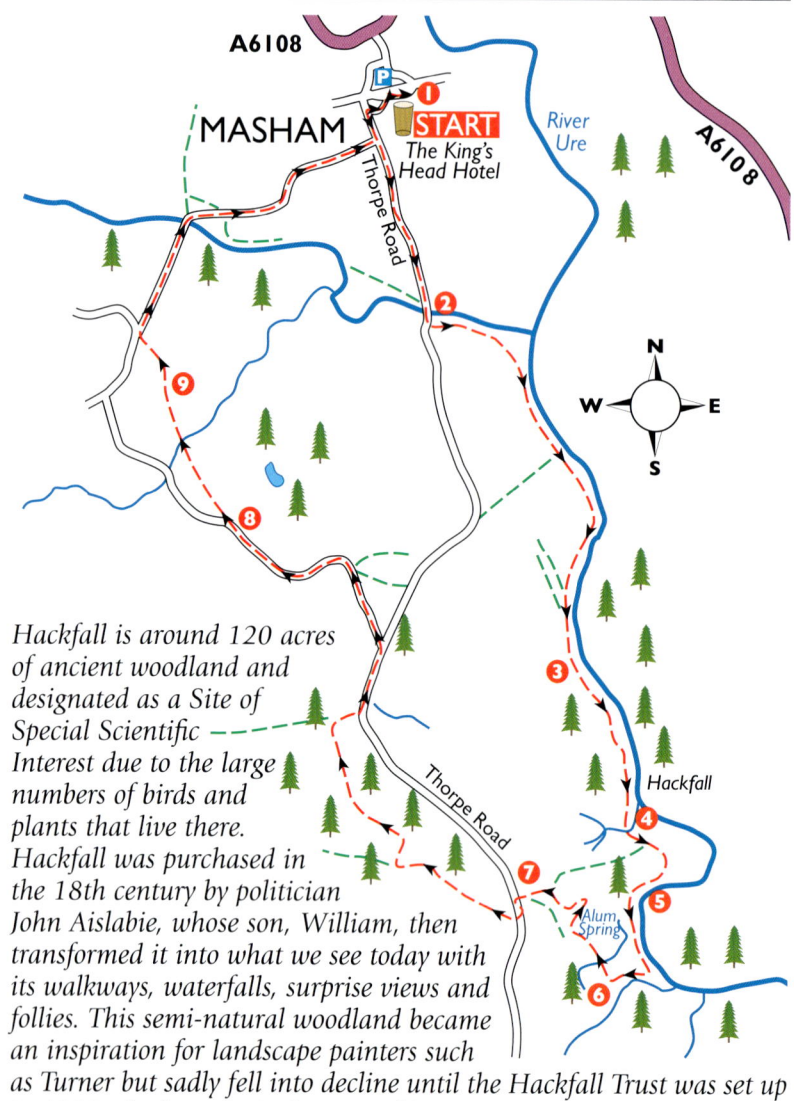

Hackfall is around 120 acres of ancient woodland and designated as a Site of Special Scientific Interest due to the large numbers of birds and plants that live there. Hackfall was purchased in the 18th century by politician John Aislabie, whose son, William, then transformed it into what we see today with its walkways, waterfalls, surprise views and follies. This semi-natural woodland became an inspiration for landscape painters such as Turner but sadly fell into decline until the Hackfall Trust was set up in 1989 who have lovingly restored it.

④ Follow the signposts for the viewpoint, heading straight on and then bearing right to reach the top of **Limehouse Hill**, where there is a gap in the trees giving a great view across the valley. Keep ahead on the path as it zigzags steeply downhill to join the river again.

Masham 15

5 Continue following the river downstream through two stone columns and then bear left on the path closest to the river, ignoring the first signpost for **Hackfall Garden Feature Walk**. Follow this riverside path for some way until you reach the second Hackfall Feature Garden signpost taking you up some steep steps to the right. At the top of the steps is **Fishers Hall**, from where there is a good view of **Hackfall** to the left and the **River Ure** to the right in the distance down below.

6 When you get to the next junction, turn right to cross **Alum Spring** and continue uphill, keeping to the left-hand path. At the next folly, the bench is positioned perfectly for a beautiful view of the steep hillside and waterfall cascading down it to the left. Continue along the path and shortly afterwards you reach **Fountains Pond**.

Fountains Pond is a pleasantly tranquil lake, surrounded by lush green foliage, created in 1756 by William Aislabie. From here you can see all the way back up to Mowbray viewpoint and Banqueting Hall high above. The most impressive part of the lake is a small island in the middle, containing a fountain hidden amongst abundant plant life. The fun part is you can operate the fountain yourself. You have to ferociously pump a handle until it spouts water up to 30 feet above the surface, but it is worth the effort as it really is quite a spectacle.

After the pond, continue on the path uphill and then at the next junction bear right to reach a wooden gate at the edge of the woodland. Cross the field diagonally to the left and uphill, to the next gate. Turn left along a stone path which takes you to a car park which you cross.

7 At the road (**Thorpe Road**) turn left, and then in 50m follow the sign to your right directing you into **Nutwith Common**. Head along the woodland path and gradually uphill for around ½ mile. At the first junction take a right to continue weaving through the trees now heading downhill. At the bottom of the woodland track turn right to reach the main road again (**Thorpe Road**). Turn left heading over the brow of the hill, and then as the road forks on the hilltop, bear left towards farm buildings. Keep along the road past the farm as it curves to the left and then right.

8 In ½ mile look for a stile on the right leading to a faint path across a field. The path isn't clear but head half-left aiming for the large trees just over the brow of the hill and you will see the next stile beside the trees. Continue in the same direction across the next two fields to two further stiles. At the stream, use the bridge which lies 40m to the left of the path. Continue heading in the same direction across the next field.

9 There are two further stiles in the corner of the next fields, and then a wooden bridge over a stream. Turn left to skirt around the edge of the next field to a signpost directing you to a road in front of **Swinton Park**. Turn right, signposted to **Masham**, and follow the road for ½ mile, over a stone bridge and past a golf course. At the T-junction turn left onto **Park Street** where you turn right along **Chapman Lane** to return to the market square.

Places of Interest Nearby

If you cannot extend the walk to encompass more of **Hackfall**, then the woodland is well worth a more focused visit on a separate occasion. The nearby village of **Grewelthorpe** has a café, an observatory, and further opportunities for exploring the outdoors, with it also being home to the award-winning **Himalayan Garden and Sculpture Park**.

Walk 16
BURNSALL & LINTON

Distance: 6¼ miles (10 km)

Start: Burnsall Car Park, Bunker's Hill, BD23 6BS.

Parking: Burnsall Car Park – the pay and display riverside car park in Burnsall.

OS Map: Explorer OL2 Yorkshire Dales – Southern & Western Areas. **Grid Ref:** SE031610.

Terrain: Mostly flat riverside paths and grassy field walking. There are lots of stiles and steps over the top of dry-stone walls, which limits how dog friendly the walk is.

Walk Tips: Grab a takeaway coffee and homemade slice of cake to take on the walk from Riverbank, a fantastic café just next to the car park at the start of the walk.

If you want to make the walk more dog friendly by avoiding the numerous stiles and dry-stone wall crossings, then this walk would still be very enjoyable as an out-and-back riverside walk.

Burnsall is a busy riverside village, very popular with Dales day-trippers in the summer months. The picturesque village is situated in a natural amphitheatre, surrounded by a circle of fells, and is known for the five-arched stone bridge which is the focal point of the village. This walk follows the River Wharfe from Burnsall to Linton, heading over both the Hebden Suspension Bridge, and the impressive Linton Falls on the way. The route

North Yorkshire Pub Walks

back leaves the river and heads more directly back to Burnsall across dry-stone-walled fields.

THE PUB **THE FOUNTAINE INN** in Linton is a traditional, stylish country pub serving food that makes use of seasonal ingredients sourced from across Yorkshire. They proudly promise "plentiful plates for hard working walkers and explorers", so you know you're in safe hands. If it's nice weather, you can take in the beautiful surroundings from the outside seating. If it's not you can settle into the cosy bar and sit by the roaring fire.
☎ 01756 752210   🌐 www.fountaineinnatlinton.co.uk

The Walk

❶ From the pay and display riverside car park, turn right and walk towards the central stone bridge. Beside it, next to the **Red Lion**'s car park entrance, there is a riverside path which you join, heading upstream. Continue to follow this path for 1 mile until you reach a narrow bridge, **Hebden Suspension Bridge**, which you cross over and then turn left to continue heading upstream.

❷ Keep following the **Dales Way** alongside the river for a further 1¼ miles. Eventually, the path leaves the riverside and you can see **Linton Church** on the other side of the river. You can cross the river using the stepping stones if you're feeling brave (and water level permitting!) or go through the gate to your right and continue in the direction of the town of **Grassington** along the country lane.

❸ In 200m, at the lane's first bend, turn left by a footpath sign directing you over the dry-stone wall to follow the river towards **Grassington** through fields. As you reach the next country lane at **Linton Falls**, you could divert right to visit the market town of **Grassington** – around ½ mile from this point to its central square. To continue the walk, turn left to cross the bridge over the top of the falls, now heading towards **Linton**.

Burnsall & Linton 16

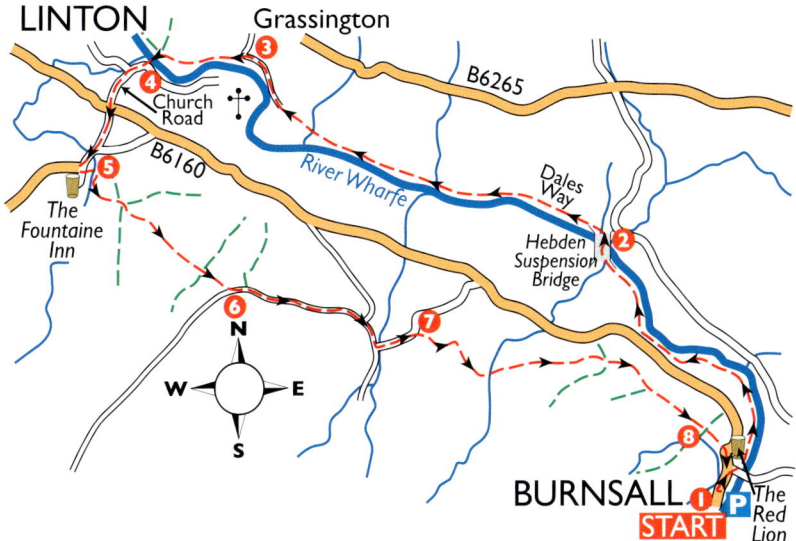

4 After crossing the bridge you reach a junction by a stream where you turn left to join the road (**Church Road**) by **Linton Falls car park**. Turn right at the road, and then at the junction by a stone bridge, keep left to continue uphill towards **Linton**. At the T-junction keep straight ahead following the sign for the **Fountaine Inn**. Cross another stone bridge in the village and you'll see the pub on the left-hand side.

5 Re-cross the river, this time on a narrow stone bridge opposite the pub. Turn right and at the end of the lane turn left to follow a footpath sign up **Thorpe Lane**. Follow the footpath sign through a gate at **Grange Farm**. The path takes you uphill through fields and past a signpost to **Threapland**, which you ignore to keep heading uphill. Pass a couple of large boulders and at the top of the hill, beside the woodland, you can see across the dip to the next footpath sign a few hundred metres in front of you at the road.

6 Cross the dry-stone wall and turn left along the narrow road. At the next road junction take a right to follow the **Way of the Roses cycle route** downhill towards the village of **Thorpe**. At the

77

next junction turn left to continue through **Thorpe** and uphill. In 200m, there is a footpath sign to **Burnsall** 1.25 miles, heading off to the right.

7 Follow this and as the trail bends, you can see the footpath sign to head for, to your right. Go into the field at the end of the track, heading downhill and through a second gate just past the next footpath sign. Follow the dry-stone wall and then a gap in the wall takes you to a wooden river crossing and subsequently across more fields. At the 5½ miles point you reach a lane which you cross to continue heading across fields on a grass path.

8 After a succession of dry-stone wall crossings, you cross straight over another farm track and then two further gates to eventually reach the road at **Burnsall**. Turn right to reach the central bridge again, where you keep right to return to your car.

Places of Interest Nearby

There are a couple of potential detour options to add to the walk if you would like to extend it. The **Old School Tea Room**, in **Hebden**, is ½ mile from **Hebden Suspension Bridge** and is well known for its coffee and delicious cake. **Grassington**, also ½ mile from the route at **Linton Falls Bridge**, is home to multiple shops and refreshment stops, and is well worth the detour.

Walk 17
Hawes & Hardraw

Distance: 5 miles (7.8 km) without a visit to Hardraw Force

Start: Gayle Lane Car Park, Hawes, DL8 3RQ.

Parking: Gayle Lane Car Park in Hawes, just next to the Primary School.

OS Map: Explorer OL30 Yorkshire Dales – Northern & Central Areas. **Grid Ref:** SD870897.

Terrain: Good terrain throughout; mostly grass paths and no hill climbing. Dog friendly.

Walk Tips: You can explore the Hardraw Force Waterfall area in numerous different ways so I would advise picking up a free map to help you with this at the entrance point.

Hawes is a bustling market town surrounded by a vast, remote area of Wensleydale countryside. This route starts in the centre of the town and heads to the small, neighbouring village of Hardraw. Here you'll find a tearoom and café, but the main attraction is without doubt Hardraw Force, England's highest unbroken waterfall.

THE PUB There are many options to choose from in the centre of Hawes, but the pick of the bunch is the **WHITE HART INN**, which retains its traditional feel with flagstone floors and wooden panelling, yet combines this with a modern high-quality menu. ☎ 01969 667214 🌐 www.whitehartawes.co.uk

North Yorkshire Pub Walks

The Walk

1 From **Gayle Lane car park** head down the steps in the far corner to the centre of **Hawes**. Directly opposite the steps, cross over **Market Place** and head down the road opposite, between two houses with a footpath sign on the right-hand house. It's only 50m to the end of the lane where you head through a driveway to the left of the end house, and through a narrow wooden gate.

2 Follow the footpath signs and path for around ¼ mile through the fields to the riverside, then turn right keeping the river on your left-hand side. In just over ¼ mile, you can see a wooden bridge in the middle of the field diagonally to your right. Cross over this bridge, and follow the path to the road just beyond.

3 Turn left and follow the road over the stone arch bridge. In 200m follow the footpath on your left, signposted **Hawes Circular Walk**. Cross the fields along the same continuous path, through a series of seven gates, following the signs to reach the road in **Hardraw** opposite **Green Dragon Inn**.

You enter the waterfall area through the Green Dragon Inn's car park, paying around £5 to enter at the Heritage Centre, which is the large building in the car park also housing a café. It is well worth the entrance fee so don't let that put you off; the 100ft single drop waterfall is the highest in England.

Once through the entrance, there are a couple of options of routes inside the waterfall's grounds. The lower path heads directly to the waterfall on a flat path. Along the way there are a couple of bridges which provide some great photo spots. The upper path climbs high out of the gorge and loops around the back of the waterfall at the top of it, but does not incorporate any waterfall views, so is the one to skip if the walk is long enough (though both can be undertaken in less than 1¼ miles combined). Simply explore the area in whichever way you like.

4 After enjoying **Hardraw Force**, retrace your steps to the road and head over the stone bridge by the side of the pub. In 100m, turn right to follow the **Pennine Way** footpath. Ignore the signpost

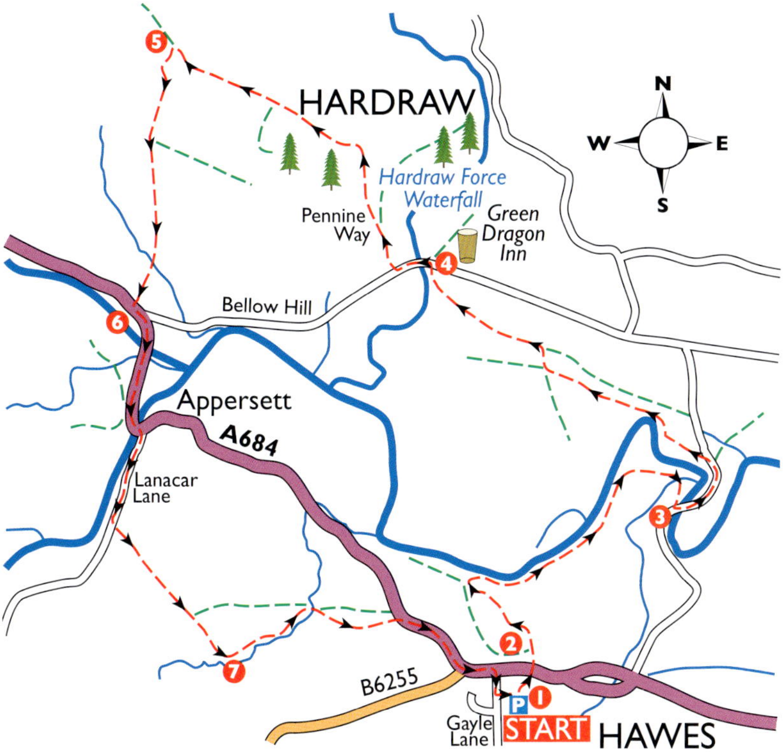

Hawes & Hardraw 17

and hole in the wall on the left after 200m and continue on the track uphill as it bends to the left beside woodland and offers you a view of the road over Buttertubs on the hillside to the right. Keep going for ¾ mile along the **Pennine Way**, until you reach a signpost on your left to **New Bridge**. Head through the gate on your left and into the field, where there is a beautiful view of the countryside ahead.

5 Ignore the track to the right and follow the dry-stone wall on your left heading downhill, to reach a ladder over the wall. Keep left again, following the path through the field, straight on at the signpost, following

81

the wooden waymarkers. You will see the path heading through two gates to meet the road.

6 Follow the road to the left and over the stone bridge. Immediately after the sign for **Appersett** and a second stone bridge, take the road (**Lanacar Lane**) to the right, heading uphill by the riverside. Immediately after **Appersett Viaduct**, take the footpath to the left over a stile, and across a field. Head through two gates, then diagonally across a field and through the third gate. The path then bends to the left by a stone barn.

7 Go through a fourth gate by a stream, and then a fifth gate heading towards farm buildings. At the farm track continue ahead to reach a road in a few hundred metres. Turn right and follow the road for the remaining ¼ mile back to Hawes, turning right at **Gayle Lane** to return to the car park.

Places of Interest Nearby

Hawes is a bustling market town, with lots of independent shops, pubs and cafés. Be sure to visit **Wensleydale Creamery** on Gayle Lane, where there is a large shop selling lots of different types of cheese, all made on site. There is also a vast array of other local Yorkshire merchandise, making it one of the best souvenir shops in the vicinity. The factory has a museum, so you can see how cheese is made first hand.

Walk 18

LEVISHAM & THE HOLE OF HORCUM

Distance: 7 miles (11.2 km)

Start: Saltergate Car Park, Lockton, YO18 7NR.

Parking: Saltergate Car Park, off the A169 Whitby Road.

OS Map: Explorer OL27 North York Moors, Eastern Area.
Grid Ref: SE852937.

Terrain: Mostly flat field and moorland tracks. The fields at the base of the Hole of Horcum can be very wet and muddy in winter, while the woodland path is also narrow, muddy and a trip hazard in places. Dog friendly.

Walk Tips: The walk can be very wet and muddy, particularly in the bowl of the Hole of Horcum. Make sure to wear appropriate footwear or reserve for a dry period.

The Hole of Horcum is a huge natural amphitheatre created over thousands of years of erosion. It is 400 ft deep and around ¾ mile across a section of the valley of Levisham Beck, and is one of the most remarkable geological sights in the North York Moors National Park. In this walk you'll make your way around its circumference, traversing the remote surrounding moorland. You'll then visit Levisham, a small village with one route in and

North Yorkshire Pub Walks

out and a cosy Yorkshire pub, the Horseshoe Inn, being the focal point. The return journey takes you through woodland and then along the bottom of the Hole of Horcum.

THE HORSESHOE INN ticks all the boxes for a quintessential, cosy Yorkshire pub; a warm welcome, a roaring fire, stone walls, and wooden tables, chairs and bar. The traditional pub fare here is of an excellent quality, and even better, they serve what are normally described as 'Yorkshire-sized portions'. There are also a few guest bedrooms should you wish to stay the night. This is the type of place where you can imagine being snowed in for days on end (and being somewhat pleased about it).
☎ 01751 460240   🌐 www.horseshoelevisham.co.uk

The Walk

❶ From **Saltergate car park** off the A169, cross over and turn right along the grassy roadside verge as it skirts around the **Hole of Horcum** on your left. The path bends downhill and at just under ½ mile you leave the road at its bend and head straight on over a stile. The path coming up from the left here from the base of the **Hole of Horcum** is the path by which you will return.

❷ Continue straight ahead on the path across the moors for 2 miles as it bends around the **Hole of Horcum**. You then meet a junction of paths and a signpost; follow the path uphill towards Levisham. Go through a gate onto a lane (**Limpsey Gate Lane**), which you then follow to reach the **Horseshoe Inn** at **Levisham**.

❸ Keep ahead through the village and in 300m, once you've passed the last house, look for a footpath sign on your left which you follow downhill into woodland. Take the left-hand path by a bench and walk for 300m until the path forks again. Take the

Levisham & the Hole of Horcum   18

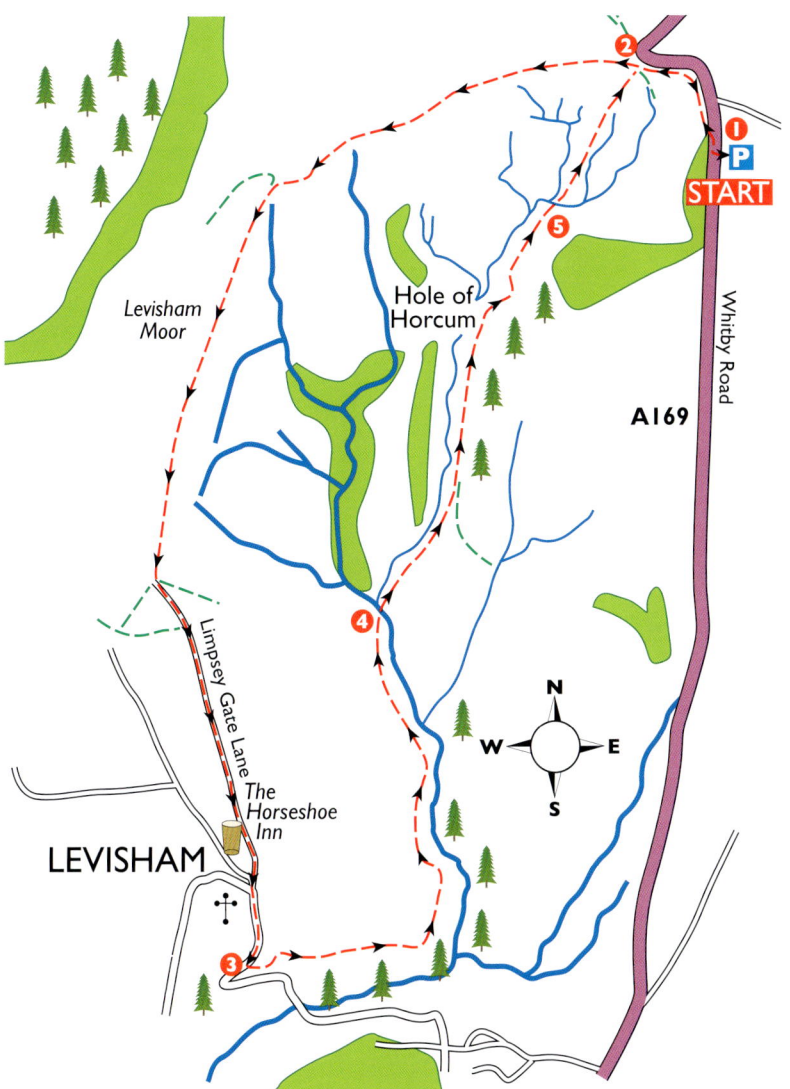

upper left path signposted for **Horcum**. Carry on skirting around the hillside on a narrow path through woodland for 1¼ miles. You then go through a gate and reach a crossroad of paths, one signposted for **Dundale Pond**, but carry on straight ahead, signposted Horcum.

North Yorkshire Pub Walks

4 The path heads over the river twice in quick succession and then continues to follow the river on a narrow path above a small valley. The path eventually heads through a gate and into fields. Keep heading in a straight line through the centre of the fields; you are now at the bottom of the **Hole of Horcum**. Just before the 6-miles mark, you pass a derelict farmhouse to your right. Keep heading in the same direction until you come to a gate at the river in the corner of the field.

5 Follow the stone path ahead which takes you on a gradual ascent out of the Hole of Horcum and back up to the road again. Follow the path which runs parallel with the road round to the right and in just under ½ mile you will be level with the car park again. Turn left and cross the road with care to return to your car.

Places of Interest Nearby

In the neighbouring village of **Lockton**, which you must pass through on any driving route to Levisham, there is **Lockton Tea Rooms and Gallery**, a modern café that is used by many as a cycling destination and brunch stop, where you will find artwork by a number of local artists on display.

Walk 19

Osmotherley & Ingleby Cross

Distance: 4 or 5½ miles (6.6 or 9 km)

Start: West End, Osmotherley, DL6 3AA.

Parking: There is roadside parking along West End just before you reach the centre of the village of Osmotherley and more available next to the Golden Lion pub a little further on.

OS Map: Explorer OL26 North York Moors, Western Area.
Grid Ref: SE453972.

Terrain: Mostly compact woodland trails and country road walking, with a short crossing of a muddy field. Some small hills to tackle. There may well be livestock in the muddy field so dogs will need to be kept on a lead here.

Walk Tips: Mount Grace Priory can easily be added to this walk as a short diversion. A look around its shop and café would add 1½ miles to the above walk on an out-and-back journey.

Although Osmotherley is situated just outside the North York Moors area it's a magnet for walkers wanting to tackle the outdoors; the village is a popular walking hub for everyone from

North Yorkshire Pub Walks

long-distance hikers to recreational dog walkers. This walk gives you an introduction to a section of both the Cleveland Way and Coast to Coast long-distance paths. The route heads from Osmotherley to the pub in Ingleby Cross in a loop, across fields and through woodland, while also offering the opportunity for a short diversion to take in the historic Mount Grace Priory.

THE PUB **THE GOLDEN LION** in Osmotherley has a great atmosphere and traditional menu. You can expect a warm welcome, a roaring fire and a good selection of draft beers.
☎ 01609 883526
🌐 www.goldenlionosmotherley.co.uk

THE PUB **THE BLUE BELL INN** in Ingleby Cross is a cosy and traditional village pub, popular with locals and visitors alike. It has a cosy bar area complete with open fires and a large rear garden, perfect for the summer months. Its reputation, excellent Sunday roast and the extremely reasonable prices make it advisable to book in advance.
☎ 01609 882272   🌐 www.thebluebellinninglebycross.co.uk

The Walk

❶ From the roadside parking in **Osmotherley**, head away from the village centre towards the A19. Turn right at a wooden signpost for a footpath and play area. Pass the play area and after ¼ mile bear right continuing along the lane to **Siddle Farm**. After 250m the track bends right into the farm but carry on following the footpath straight on and into the field. Cross the field to reach a stile directly ahead.

At this point you can add a diversion to visit Mount Grace Priory should you wish to. To make the diversion, after crossing the stile, head downhill to the left following the fence line and in the bottom left corner you reach woodland where there is another stile. Simply follow the path through the woodland for ½ mile to **Mount Grace Priory***.*

Osmotherley & Ingleby Cross 19

2 To continue the walk, turn right through the field and then a farm gate and head steeply uphill to another gate at the top of the field. Keep heading uphill towards the stone stable where you will see a footpath sign directing you through another wooden gate. As you pass the farm barns you will see the **Cleveland Way** signpost ahead. Take the left path through the gate, following the footpath sign, not heading uphill along the dry-stone wall. After ½ mile you will see another signpost and junction of gates. Head to the left downhill following the **Coast to Coast** path. On your return journey you will however head uphill here following the sign for **Lady Chapel**.

3 After 200m downhill, leave the **Coast to Coast** path to carry on straight ahead along the forest track. After around ½ mile on this track, take the wooden steps on the left taking you off the track and steeply down into the woodland on a footpath. Follow the footpath signposted through the woodland and then take a right when you meet a track at the bottom of the woodland after 300m.

4 If you don't wish to head to the **Blue Bell Inn** jump to point 5. However, if you are visiting the pub turn right and after another 300m on this track turn left to keep heading downhill. You then come to a lane after 200m, where you turn right. In ½ mile you will reach the A172, which you cross with care. The **Blue Bell Inn** is 100m further up the road on the left in **Ingleby Cross**. After your pub stop, retrace the ¾ mile back up the **Coast to Coast** path to where you came out of the woodland on to the

North Yorkshire Pub Walks

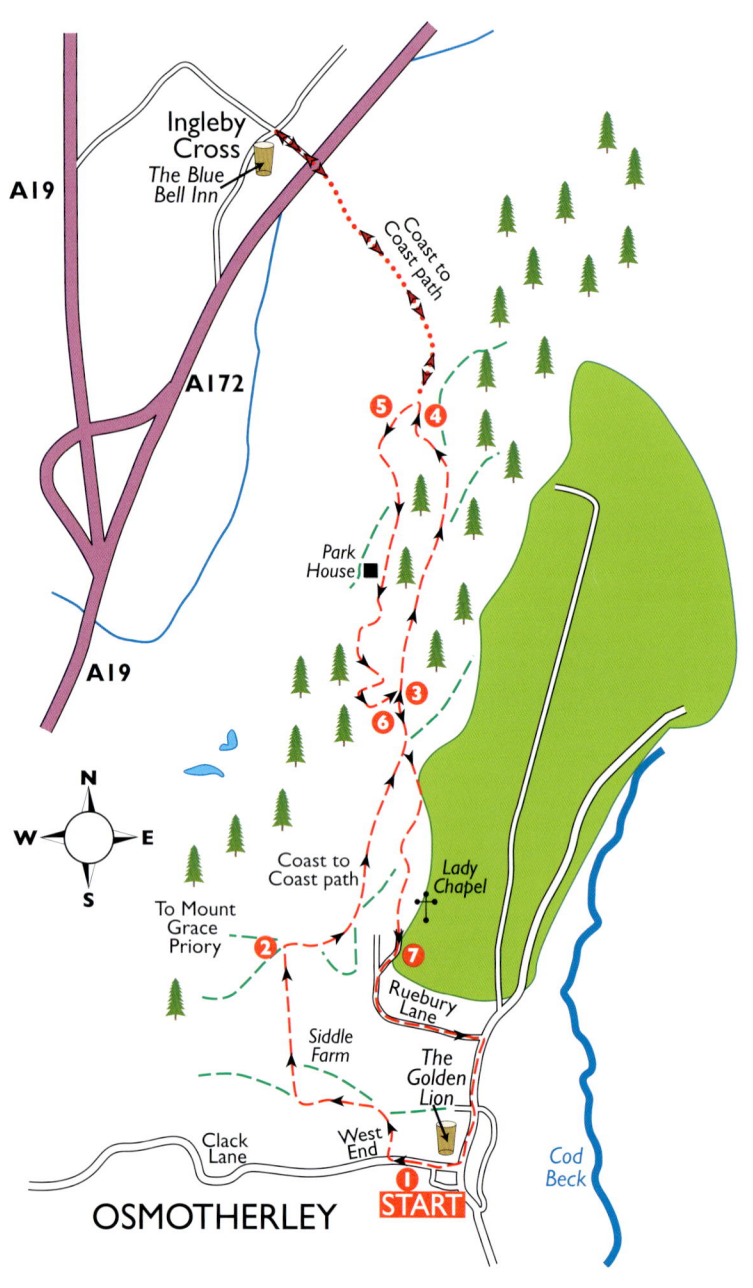

Osmotherley & Ingleby Cross

forest track. This time however, head straight on, and follow the **Coast to Coast** path along this track until you reach the signpost you saw on the way out.

5 To continue the walk turn left here (keep right along this path if you have visited the pub). You will pass **Park House**, a B&B with an honesty-box tuck shop outside for passing walkers. Keep left at the fork and continue following the **Coast to Coast** path uphill. The path twists and turns through the woodland and eventually you join a path you walked earlier in the route. Turn right here and in 200m you will reach the junction of gates which you saw on your outward journey. This time you take a left and follow the **Cleveland Way** uphill.

6 After 100m uphill, head through the gate and continue to follow the **Cleveland Way**. After 100m you will see a signpost to **Lady Chapel** off to the left, uphill. Take this path and walk through the grounds of **Lady Chapel** (if you wish to look inside, the door is often left open and visitors are welcome).

7 Once through the chapel's grounds there are steps heading to a lane which you continue to follow downhill for 300m, past miniature wooden crosses on the left. The lane then joins another country lane (**Ruebury Lane**), which you follow for 300m past houses to reach the road into **Osmotherley**. Turn right and walk the remaining ¼ mile past the village store and then right along **West End** to return to your car.

Places of Interest Nearby

Mount Grace Priory, House and Gardens is run by English Heritage and is home to the best preserved Carthusian priory in England. Here you can explore the ruins of the medieval monastery and roam the recently renovated gardens. However, if you don't have much time to spare, a visit to the café and gift shop still make it worth the trip.

If you're looking for another walk in the area then take the 1½ mile stroll around **Cod Beck Reservoir**. This man-made lake just near Osmotherley village has a mostly flat, well surfaced path around it making it great for all-weather walking.

Walk 20

KETTLEWELL & STARBOTTON

Distance: 4½ miles (7.3 km)

Start: Yorkshire Dales National Park Car Park, Kettlewell, BD23 5QZ.

Parking: Yorkshire Dales National Park Car Park is a pay and display car park in the centre of Kettlewell village.

OS Map: Explorer OL30 Yorkshire Dales – Northern & Central Areas. **Grid Ref:** SD967722.

Terrain: Mostly flat field path walking, but lots of stiles and gates over dry-stone walls, which somewhat limits how dog friendly this walk is.

Walk Tips: Check the Fox & Hounds' winter opening hours before setting off. If they don't suit your plans, there are further pub options in Kettlewell, as well as two cafés.

Centrally located in the Dales, the quintessential Yorkshire village of Kettlewell is something of a hub for Dales tourism and walking. The village's main road is one of few roads that cuts north to south through the beautiful Dales countryside

Kettlewell & Starbotton

and valley of Upper Wharfedale, making the village a hive of activity. Kettlewell is also the starting point for many of Upper Wharfedale's finest walks. This walk initially climbs above the village to offer an impressive vantage point of Upper Wharfedale, and then simply follows the valley across fields to the next village of Starbotton, before returning alongside the river in the base of the valley.

THE FOX & HOUNDS in Starbotton is an old, traditional family-run pub with flagstone floors, an open fire and a small beer garden at the front. Featured in CAMRA's *Good Beer Guide*, the pub is popular with locals and walkers alike.

☎ 01756 760269
🌐 www.foxandhoundsstarbotton.co.uk

THE BLUE BELL INN is perfectly situated in the centre of Kettlewell and serves hearty, home-cooked food and locally brewed ales. Dog friendly.
☎ 01756 760 230   🌐 www.bluebellkettlewell.com

The Walk

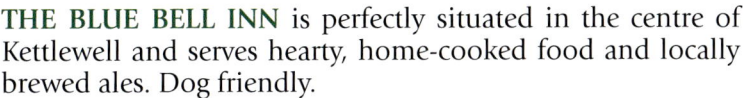

1 From the car park, turn left, cross over the stone bridge and head towards the **Blue Bell Inn**. Turn right down **Far Lane**, behind the pub. When the road bends round to the right, keep ahead on the footpath heading steeply uphill and passing the **Kettlewell Weather Stone**. After 50m cross over the dry-stone wall and turn left to walk along the hillside on the faint path with wonderful views of Kettlewell behind you and the valley to your left.

2 Follow this path through fields, sparse woodland and numerous gates and stile crossings of dry-stone walls for 1½ miles. After passing through yet another gate across a dry-stone wall, the path eventually stops heading along the valley and turns to the left downhill.

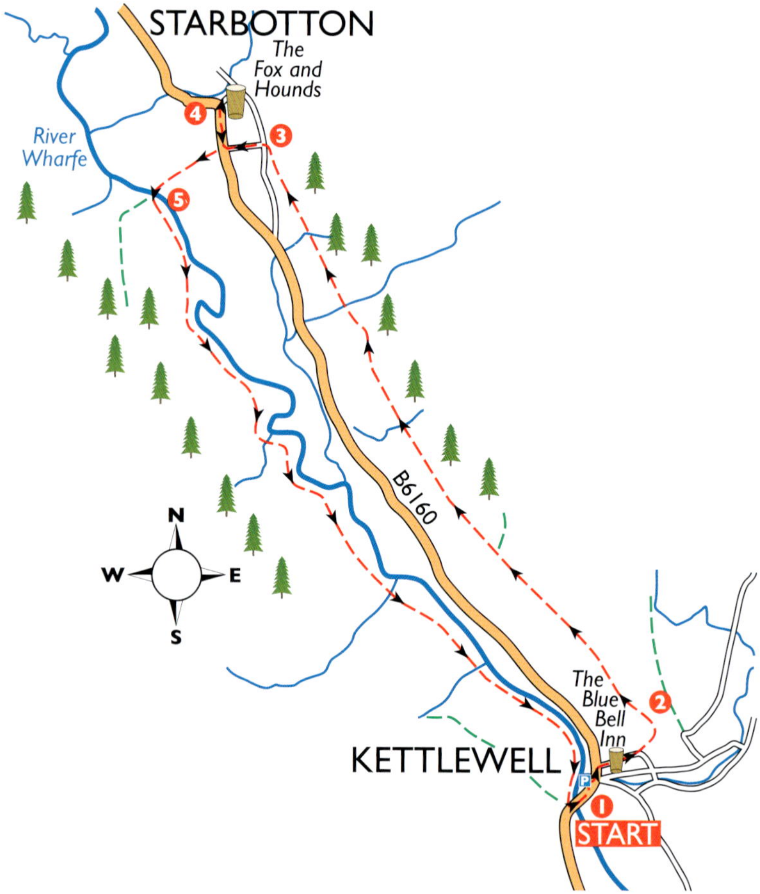

North Yorkshire Pub Walks

Kettlewell & Starbotton

❸ Continue to make your way to **Starbotton** through the field downhill and following the public footpath signs. At the road, turn right and then bear left to join the main road from Kettlewell to Starbotton. Turn right and in 100m you'll reach the **Fox and Hounds** pub in Starbotton, at the 2¼ mile mark.

❹ From the front of the pub, retrace your steps back along the main road, passing the junction you emerged from. After another 50m and level with the field which you came downhill through to meet the road, look to your right for a signpost for Arncliffe, Kettlewell and Buckden. Go through the gate to take this path heading slightly downhill and towards the river.

❺ Cross the river on the wooden bridge and then take a left and continue to head back towards Kettlewell. Follow the riverside path across the fields sticking to the **Dales Way** all the way back to meet the road at Kettlewell. Turn left over the stone road bridge to return to the car park and the centre of **Kettlewell**.

Places of Interest Nearby

The valley of **Upper Wharfedale**, in which both Kettlewell and Starbotton are situated, is a popular base for a number of hill walks, including family-friendly **Great Whernside**, the sixth-highest peak in the Dales (not to be confused with Whernside – one of the Yorkshire Three Peaks) and Buckden Pike, which takes you past waterfalls and an abandoned lead mine.

OTHER TITLES FROM COUNTRYSIDE BOOKS

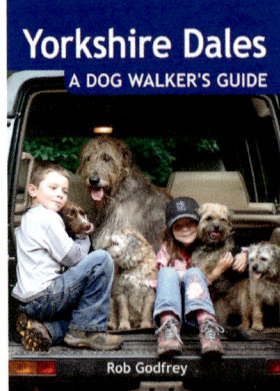

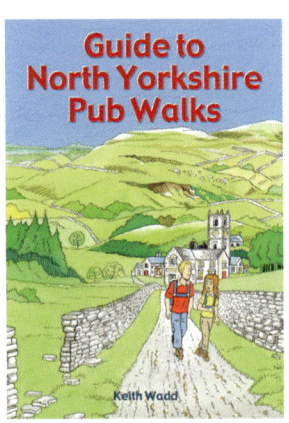
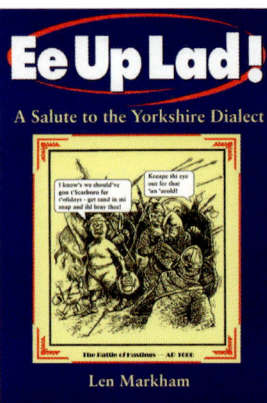
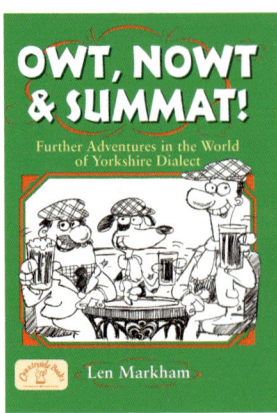
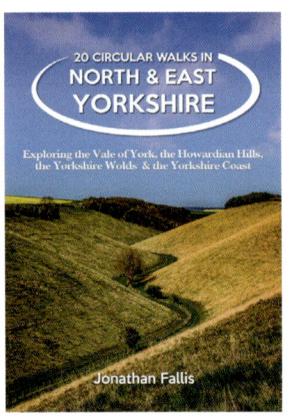
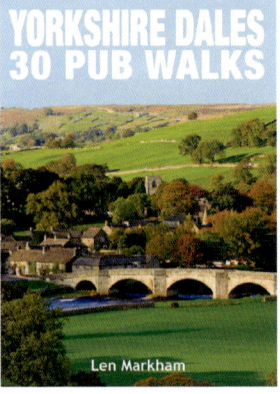
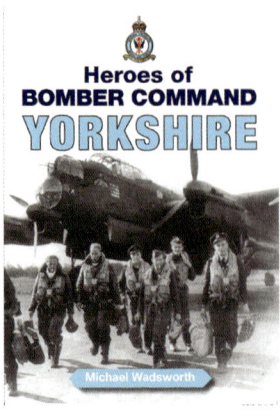

To see the full range of books by Countryside Books please visit
www.countrysidebooks.co.uk

Follow us on   @CountrysideBooks